Print ISBN-13: 978-1-7341489-1-6
E-book ISBN-13: 978-1-7341489-0-9
Library of Congress Control Number: 2020912477

Disclaimer:
Every effort has been made to ensure that the information in this book was correct at press time, the author and publisher do not assume and hereby disclaim any liability to any party for any loss, damage, or disruption caused by errors or omissions, whether such errors or omissions result from negligence, accident, or any other cause.

This book is not intended as a substitute for the medical advice of physicians or psychologists. The reader should regularly consult professionals for matters relating to his/her mental health.

Angela Sue Garvey
www.angelasue.com

tiny homes & tummy tucks

A SPIRITUAL DOWNSIZING

ANGELA SUE GARVEY

Contents

Join the Facebook group to discuss
how you can downsize to rightsize.

https://www.facebook.com/groups/aspiritualdownsizing

Website: angelasue.com
Facebook: facebook.com/AngelaSueGarvey
Instagram: instagram.com/AngelaSueGarvey

Disclaimer: I did my best to write events and conversations from my memory and point of view. I'm sure others would have a different perspective, and I've tried my best to tell my story without sharing someone else's. I've changed some names and identifying details to maintain the privacy of certain people. I do not intend to misrepresent any person, community, group, or organization.

For My Love, Jeff, who carried me
as I processed the trauma of abuse
and through the shifting seas of my faith,
all the while sharing in the
mourning and healing of both.

"Yearning for a new way will not produce it. Only ending the old way can do that. You cannot hold onto the old all the while declaring that you want something new. The old will defy the new; the old will deny the new; the old will decry the new. There is only one way to bring in the new. You must make room for it."

-Neale Donald Walsch

Introduction

This is the story of a kitchen junk drawer. It didn't start as a junk drawer but a place to keep the lids of mason jars. Over time, I added a few things here and there: pens, nails from photo frames, sippy cup straws, zip ties, bag clips, and safety pins. Any little thing I wasn't sure about went into the drawer until one day, I couldn't fit anything else. It was at its limit, and I was forced to take everything out of the drawer and sort it. Deciding what I was going to keep or toss. Only this was not just a junk drawer, this was my life, and it was coming apart at the seams with stuff.

I spent my life collecting things to fill all the rooms in my house — furniture, photos, clothes, decorations, dishes. Pretty things, practical things, presents from others. Some things were cheap, and some very costly. I would sit in my four-bedroom, three-bathroom house, surrounded by stuff. A quick inventory revealed over 50 frames hanging up, 16 places to sit downstairs alone, hundreds of books, and over 300 clothes hangers for my family of four and at least half of those belonged to yours truly. The laundry was always full, the dishes never all the way done, and the weeds didn't stop growing.

Maybe the most important things I collected were things you couldn't put a price on. Early morning coffee at my parent's house, chats with my girlfriends, gooey baby kisses, and big life lessons. And for better or worse, I accumulated ideas on the world and beliefs about God. I mulled over the bad advice given to me at the hands of well-intentioned church leaders. On Sundays, I would perch myself on a wooden church pew, trying to force my heart, but feeling nothing but disdain for the church who grew me. As much as I wanted to let it go, I gripped the contempt like an exhausted soldier clutches a canteen in the hot desert sand. It became my lifeline. I pondered my belonging in the church, and I held tightly to the belief I was nothing more than the red-headed stepchild of Christianity.

I polished my cynicism until it sparkled and flowed into other areas as I gathered taxing parenting advice, hurtful conversations, and gossip. I amassed for myself family drama, broken relationships, and my failed marriage. I hoarded jealousy and insecurity and excess expectations. Most of these things I never consciously planned on collecting. I didn't even realize I had brought them home for keeps. They just found me. I could never physically touch any of these things, but I was buckling from the strain of their weight. Everywhere I went, in every conversation, and at every turn, it was all there anchoring down my heart.

And I was thoroughly defeated.

I willed myself to get it together. Oh man, I knew it could be different. My put-together-self would be holy and loved, and at her core, she would know she was a child of God. And her life, well, that would be amazing too. She would whip up delicious treats in her spotless kitchen and have wild sex every night. She wouldn't need Spanx or wrinkle cream, and her student loans would be paid off. But if all this weren't possible, I would settle for learning to let a few things go. To set down the bowling balls I was juggling.

A while back, my three-year-old was being way too quiet. Eerily quiet. I was enjoying the peace until I realized he was up to something, as quiet kids always are. I found him in our pantry, holding the shiny red fire extinguisher. The white powder was everywhere. Before I lost it (and I did), I did what every millennial mom does - grabbed my phone to snap a photo. Only there was no space left on my phone. It was full. It said, "Go to settings to manage storage."

That's where my life was. Full. Maxed out. So I went to my life settings and managed my storage. I deleted it all and made space. I called it my Quitting Practice because it's not so much a one-time thing as something to be practiced.

I became curious about what would happen if I said no more to the expectations, insecurities, and daily routines I had collected without giving them much thought. What if I let my arms drop all the things I had collected so I could reclaim joy, belonging, and my self worth? What if I quit it all?

Maybe you're thinking, "Quitters never prosper. Successful people don't give up. There's shame in giving up." But there is a vast difference between giving up and quitting.

Giving up is a result of not finding the right way. It's like when you make a New Year's Resolution to lose weight and then by January 10th you are completely off course. You didn't wake up and say, *today I'm going to give up.* It just kind of happens as a co-worker brings a pink box of donuts to the office, and you've sucked down two jelly-filled before the first meeting. You do it without really thinking.

Quitting is a calculated choice to stop doing something for a specific reason. Giving up is about caving; quitting is about conviction. It's a declaration that you are going in a different direction to honor yourself, your family, and God. It's about clearing the decks to add in what makes a life worth living.

So I laid my clutter across the floor and began to untangle the mass of stuff in my life. Everything that has misshapen my direction and allowed me to drift into a land of spiritual unconnectedness and overwhelm.

And I quit.

All of it.

1. Quit Walking on Eggshells

"Please stop!" I screamed.

His eyes were fixed, and he was laughing.

"Why are you doing this?" I frantically grabbed the passenger dashboard.

He forcefully laid on the gas pedal. It was dark, but I could see we were accelerating our car right towards a young mom behind the wheel of a small sedan with her precious baby in a car seat.

"No!" I squeezed my eyes shut, but I'll never forget that horrified mom's face as she rushed and just barely got out of the way.

He laughed again, lightly this time, seeming satisfied that I was shaking uncontrollably.

Like many other nights, I cried myself to sleep alone. How did I get here? I needed help.

The first time I decided to quit something, I was twenty-years old, in an awkward adolescent phase, and still living at home. My parents and I had a relationship most parents dream about. We never had the typical rough teenage years and genuinely enjoyed being around each other, but we had just moved to a new town, and stress was higher for us all. I was struggling to adjust and needed space to stretch my wings and perhaps fall a few times and learn how to get back up on my own. One night after an emotionally charged fight, I packed a duffel bag and recoiled to my best friend's couch. She was a newlywed, and I wasn't fond of her husband because he had a wandering eye. She hadn't noticed yet. He knew exactly how little I thought of him so I couldn't stay long. But in my rebellion, I didn't want to go home. I was going to make it on my own.

At the time, I had been dating Trevor, a Marine I met line dancing, and he was helping me search for an apartment. He was charming and funny and suggested getting a place together. It had only been a few months, but I was craving the freedom of being on my own, the romance of sharing my life with someone, and mostly I wanted to be a grown-up. Plus, I couldn't keep sleeping on my girlfriend's couch. Without my parent's blessing and against my Christian upbringing, I said yes, and at the end of January, we moved in together.

We shopped for new couches and a bar-height kitchen table with seating for four. We found artwork to hang with 20% off Bed Bath and Beyond coupons and a large geometric rug from Target to style the little apartment. We both were enthusiastic as we unpacked, but I noticed Trevor was over assertive about finding the perfect place for everything, making sure his shoes were always perfectly lined up in the closet, and all the frames hung perfectly straight. Perfect being the central theme. In the first few days, I noticed his anxiousness about things being just right. I brushed it off because moving is stressful. Until one week in, we got into an awful fight. His temper took me off guard, how quickly his eyes turned cold, and the meanness that appeared, but this was my first grown-up relationship.

I didn't know how fights were supposed to go. My parents don't really fight. They got married young, 16 and 19 years young, and have been together for over 50 years. I'm sure they disagree at times, but in all my years I've never seen them fight in front of me. I was in uncharted territory. Experts say arguing is normal and healthy. Were name-calling and door slamming normal fighting? I had no idea. I'd never seen it played out. All I knew was that only a week in, I was sitting on my bedroom floor with salty tears running down my cheeks and a bruised ego, wondering what I'd gotten myself into. I clearly had made a mistake but didn't know how to fix it. Not because I signed a 12-month lease but because I didn't want to crawl back to my family and admit I was wrong about moving in with Trevor. I cautiously accepted his apology and tried to forget it ever happened.

In June, at a shabby commercial chapel, smack dab in the middle of an Auto Zone and a nail salon, we eloped. I immediately regretted it. I felt overwhelming shame for not including my family, and my insecurity was skyrocketing because, for weeks, he didn't want to tell anyone we got married. Or that he was off the market. After our shotgun wedding, he dropped the news that he had been married before and might have a son, which he didn't know for sure, he casually explained, because she ran out on him. It was pretty much her fault, and the boy most likely wasn't his, he said. I was speechless. After the shock settled in, I dug around and found her MySpace page and pictures of a sweet little boy, a tiny little carbon copy of Trevor. My heart dropped.

About a month later, against Trevor's wishes, I confessed my marriage to my family. My parents were loving and supportive and never once tried to make me feel guilty. They even sounded happy for me. But one of my brothers was angry.

"Why would you do something so stupid!" He yelled through the phone.

"I'm not asking for your approval. I just thought you'd want to know."

"You're such a disappointment to our family."

I heard the phone click off.

Like a dark shadow, the shame I held for getting married in secret followed me for the next few years and played a part in why I stayed longer than I should have.

Life went on, and I would see Trevor's temper come up, always displaying the same pattern. Things would set him off, and he would yell at me or sometimes break things and then apologize. I never reached out for help from my family or friends because I know it takes two to fight, and I'm not even close to perfect. One of my friends would talk to us about all her marriage problems and her awful husband. Every time she would forgive him and pretend it was all fine. But we all hated him. And I didn't want my family to hate Trevor. I stayed silent. I covered for all the bad moods, fits of anger, broken cell phones, and the huge hole he punched in my wall.

One day, he kicked in our bedroom door, splitting the entire door down the middle. Later that week, my mom stopped by. As she walked towards the bathroom, she noticed the broken door.

"What happened here?"

I felt a little lightheaded. "A strong wind blew the door shut, and it just cracked in half." (Because that happens, right?)

My mom looked concerned, "Honey, are you okay?"

"I'm fine, just a little scattered from school and work."

"Okay. Well, if you need anything, I'm here."

I think she believed me because I'm naturally strong and outspoken. I'm not sure I met anyone's perception of an abused woman.

The thing about abuse that makes it confusing is half the fights are typical, run-of-the-mill marriage stuff. And I take responsibility for my part. But it's the other half - the yelling, breaking things, belittling - those things blur the lines. More and more, little things set him off, especially when I would forget to clean something. Once, I left a used Starbucks cup and the empty straw wrapper in the car because when I had walked into the house, my hands were full of things I was unloading, and I forgot about the cup.

He went to use the car to run an errand but saw the trash and yelled for me to come into the garage.

"You never take care of the things I buy you!" he yelled, throwing the cup on the floor.

"My hands were full," I explained, "and it's just a Starbucks cup."

This only fueled him. "I don't ask for much!"

I watched in dread as he gave me a jaw-clenched lecture on how I should care for our things. His anger was my fault. I was the one pushing his buttons. I know this because it's what he repeatedly told me. It wouldn't be happening if I could just pull it together and stop making him so mad.

"Nobody else makes me as angry as you do," he would tell me.

At this point, if you're wondering why I didn't leave, I'm right there with you. When I write these words, I think it too. Who in their right mind would stay? But I wasn't in my right mind. They say if you put a frog in boiling water, it would jump right out. But if you put the frog in cold water and slowly turn up the temperature, the frog can't tell and gets cooked to death. And that's what being in a controlling relationship is like, slowly over time the heat rises and you don't know what's normal anymore.

I held a stigma that if it's not physical damage, the kind that leaves you wearing turtlenecks and sunglasses to hide bruises, then it's not abuse. I could write about the time he nearly broke my fingers for trying to change the radio station or "jokingly" waved a knife at me while I screamed for him to stop, but this was the exception for me. Mostly it was the underpinnings of cutting words and controlling with threats of outbursts, always followed by a meaningless, cold-eyed apology. It's taken me years to see that verbal and emotional abuse is still abuse. It's tough because there's usually no bruising to prove it. There is never a single moment when a bruise is acceptable. But harsh words can't be easily measured.

My self-esteem delicately strangled like a campfire under soft rain. It started with a few backhanded comments about his gorgeous ex-girlfriends, too-long glances at women we would walk past, or the constant sound of his cell phone ringing with calls from his ex-girlfriends. Yet, he swore up-and-down he wasn't talking to them and had no idea why they were calling. I started questioning my beauty and intelligence, comparing myself to every woman I came across. I felt needy and jealous and a shadow of the strong woman I was when we met.

Seven months into our marriage, on Valentine's Day weekend, we rented a log cabin in Big Bear, California with Emily, one of my best friends, and her boyfriend. Emily and I met when we were eight years old at the local YMCA daycare and became instant best friends. Soul sisters. We bonded over our love for cooking and all the boys in *Teen Beat* magazine. Since we were little, we dreamed of the day we would be grown up enough to fall in love and start a family, side-by-side. We planned everything to make this trip perfect. We had outings and games, but we were most passionate about our menu for Saturday night: Italian Stuffed Flank Steak with garlic, prosciutto, and provolone next to roasted fingerling potatoes. For dessert, we were making her mom's famous berry trifle recipe. When we arrived at the cabin Friday night, Trevor and I unloaded our things, and he drove us into the town to explore.

Just a few blocks into the town, his phone started to ring non-stop. He silenced it, but someone kept calling. I was pretty sure it was Sophie, his ex-girlfriend from Alabama, whom he swore he hadn't talked to in months.

"You can answer it." I dared him.

He ignored me and silenced it again.

My bull-shit meter was sending Mayday signals. The air was thin, and my voice pinched.

"If you have nothing to hide, let me see it!" I reached for his phone.

He yanked his flip phone back, and with calm hands, he cracked it in half. His eyes were dead cold.

"Stop being such an insecure bitch."

Then, while he was still driving, he rolled his window down and threw the phone out.

I sat silently, not knowing what to say.

Back at the cabin, I spent the rest of the weekend awkwardly hiding our argument from Emily because I didn't want to ruin her romantic weekend. Trevor and I made it through dinner, and immediately after the berry trifle, we excused ourselves to our room where we didn't speak.

I had no idea what to do next. I never wanted to play detective in marriage, but once we got home, I unhinged my internal Nancy Drew. I sat at his computer and logged into his cell phone account, opened the call history, and froze. He *was* still talking to Sophie. In fact, he had never stopped talking to her. My vision was fuzzy. I blinked a few times to make sure I saw right. I scanned the ledger again. I saw perfectly. And it wasn't just her. He was talking to all his exes. Not only a few quick calls but hundreds of calls, some lasting hours. The ones he promised he had stopped communicating with. The ones he said I was crazy and insecure for even thinking he was talking to.

All of them.

My brain couldn't process this. I would have stood up to leave, but my head was spinning, and my body cemented in the chair. A little more research on his computer, and I uncovered his profile on a dating website with a relationship status of "committed but looking." It was actually a relationship status option to pick. Committed. *But looking.*

It should have been the end of our marriage, but he made big promises. We reached out to our church for guidance and joined a marriage group. They were studying the book, *His Needs, Her Needs:*

Building an Affair-Proof Marriage by Willard F. Harley. We bought a copy. Despite the slight infidelity, the church encouraged us to work through it because, as the pastor assured us, "All good marriages struggle, but with faith and by giving your marriage to God, you can allow God to fix it." Apparently, I only needed a stronger faith and to get out of God's way. Or as Christians like to say, "Let go and let God."

We pressed on until that night driving home when my husband hit the gas pedal and barreled purposefully towards a young mom with her baby in the back seat. She barely made it to safety, and he just laughed.

2. Downsizing Marriage

A few weeks later, we were sitting in a tiny church office on old green chairs made of itchy wool, trying to get marriage advice from a pastor of a large, popular church we were attending. They extended counseling because this is where you go when your life is in trouble. You don't turn to a psychologist or licensed counselor. You turn to your pastor. Head of the church. Leader of the Flock.

I attempted to describe my efforts. How much I wanted, needed, our marriage to work, but I was at a loss. I didn't know what else to do. The name-calling, the short fuse, and the fear of him raging and breaking things were too high. I was weary. Too empty to tread lightly. Too tired of walking on eggshells. I pointed to the obsessive-compulsive way he walks in the front door and immediately examines the carpet for vacuum lines and disparages me if they were missing.

Just a few days before the counseling appointment, after one of our fights, like a crazed lady, or perhaps a desperate one in an abusive relationship, I had taken pictures of our home because it was very tidy. I knew if someone else, hopefully this pastor, would look at my house, look at these photos, they would point out the unreasonableness because nothing was ever out of place. But sadly, it didn't happen.

The pastor held up his hand, signaling me to stop. His expression was scolding, as if I was tattling on my kid brother for stealing my favorite toy.

"No, no. I can't look at those photos."

I tensed, very hesitant to hear what was coming next.

"I can't see in a photo if there is dust, and really, you need to be cleaning the way your husband wants the house to be clean." He recited the verse about wives submitting to their husbands "as unto the Lord."

I was to obey and quit being difficult because the wife should be a helper to her husband. Trevor's success in work and life was dependent on me playing my part as the good wife.

With a smug grin on his face, Trevor sat taller.

Disheartened, I sat through the rest of the meeting perplexed. I fell silent, so I didn't elicit more biblical advice. The pastor never addressed the more significant issue of his anger problem — not one measly word. As we stepped out of the office, he stopped us in the doorway.

"Here, take this."

He handed Trevor a trifold pamphlet on "How to Control Your Anger." The pastor gave him a pat on the back as if to say, "Good luck with your woman." and then glanced at me and said, "Don't forget to read your new marriage book."

I'm sure the trifold pamphlet had the most transcendent, brilliant advice, that undoubtedly would have stitched our marriage up like a sock puppet, but we never found out. It remained in the glove box unread until Trevor threw it out because we certainly don't keep trash in the car. I couldn't see it at the time, but this would become a pivotal moment in my relationship with the Christian church and church leadership. Not only did the church not protect, recognize, or condemn abuse in my marriage, but they supplied advice that furthered the abuse and coated it with words like submissiveness.

Financially, we were overextended, and the scarcity of cash flow added to the mounting pressure in our marriage. Trevor thought the answer was for him to take a job overseas for nine months. I wasn't sure what was going to happen in my marriage but agreed he should take the job. I was so knocked down and heartbroken and wildly needed relief from this marriage pressure cooker. He was eager to go and, I reasoned, it would be beneficial for both of us. He took the job, and I moved into my old room at my parent's house.

With Trevor gone, I spent time with friends and family whom I called less and less while working to repair my marriage. Each passing day lifted some of the heaviness I was lugging around and, not being in the day-to-day yuckiness of a downward spiraling relationship, my spirit rose. I found laughter and play, and I relaxed into my new life, married but alone. I found a solid church to attend and started counseling on my own, this time with a real psychologist, not a church pastor. I couldn't risk being hurt again by someone untrained or unwilling to recognize abuse.

My counselor, a late 50's guy named Tom, had a gray beard and wore flip-flops. He spent the first half of his life running a badge and gun before he retired as a police lieutenant. He had seen all kinds of abusive relationships, both back when he patrolled the streets, and now in this very office I occupied. Over the next few months, we worked to process my life and relationships and my feeble marriage. I'm forever thankful for Tom. I knew my marriage couldn't operate with only me trying, yet I had no idea how to convince Trevor to come to counseling.

One night, a few weeks after he went overseas, I dialed Trevor's cell phone and heard a raspy, woman's voice. Unquestionably, I had just woken her.

"Hello?" she whispered.

"Who is this?" I demanded.

She immediately hung up on me. My body felt suspended over a bridge. My fingers trembled as I redialed. No answer. Unstable and distraught, I must have dialed back 100 times, and nobody ever picked up. I couldn't sleep. Over and over again, I kept hearing that raspy voice asking, *"Hello?"* in my mind. I couldn't get a hold of Trevor until the next day. He swore it was his roommate's girlfriend. She found his phone during a party and answered. He was mad with my probing, "This is all in your head. You're too insecure." And this part was true. I was insecure.

The infidelity signs were all there, like party balloons tied to a mailbox welcoming me to the end of my marriage. But irrationally I needed concrete proof, to see with my own eyes. I needed a smoking gun. Nobody would say I didn't try hard enough. On the phone, I told him if we were going to make this marriage work, we needed to go to counseling together. He resisted. I asserted it was a deal-breaker for me. He reluctantly agreed. Over the next few weeks, I spent hours carefully reading and highlighting dozens of marriage books, seeking the answers we needed. But if I'm honest, deep down, I knew this was the beginning of the end.

The week before he came home, my anxiety peaked. I unraveled from happy-go-lucky to full-on Bride of Chucky. I looked for anything that was a potential trigger for conflict and worked to head it off. I cleaned and straightened and organized. Now living with my parents, my mom noticed my antsiness. Trevor traveled home, and at our first joint counseling appointment, Tom gave us number 2 pencils we used to fill in bubbles on a lengthy, intrusive questionnaire about our marriage. Everything from our hobby inclinations to spiritual tenets, to money management.

After an hour, we put our pencils down and left. We fought as we drove back to my parents.

Stepping out of the car, he shouted at me in the driveway.
"You're such a bitch."

My body was shaking, which I hated. It always shakes when I'm anxious, completely betraying my attempt to pretend everything was fine, as my neighbors looked on from their garage. I went to open the car to retrieve my purse from the back seat when I heard the car beep. Trevor had locked the car door, on purpose. I looked up, and his cold eyes bore into me. I stood there. My mouth was gaping, but nothing came out. Then he turned and strolled into the house, leaving me standing alone and unable to get my purse. I looked at the ground as I walked towards the house to avoid my neighbors' concerns. I'm pretty sure they heard it all. I was humiliated.

The fighting was easy to hide when we lived far away but not so much living with my parents. We planned to find our own place quickly, but I hesitated to leave the safety of my parent's house. In the nine months I was without him, I rebuilt my strength and gathered enough seeds of courage to stand up for myself. I started to push back more, which created more tension in my marriage. Trevor seemed more bothered than usual. We weren't connecting at all. A few days after the counseling appointment, I learned why.

I was getting ready for the day, showering, and getting dressed. I walked back into the bedroom, and I caught him typing a long email. Before he noticed I was looking over his shoulder, I saw her name. It was raspy-voice woman.

"What's this?" I said, startling him.

He turned, saw me glaring at the screen, and sprang up from the chair, simultaneously hitting the power button. The entire computer shut down.

"What is going on? Who is she?"

My questions angered him. He flipped the desk chair over, and his fist came down on the keyboard drawer, and he said terrible words.

Broken keyboard. Broken heart. Broken marriage.

My last battle had just ended. I was done. We were done. I simply needed to tell him. Only it didn't seem so simple. After things cooled off, we walked to the neighborhood park to talk. The park was empty. The air was thick. It was October and still ninety degrees. He sat on the bench. My heart was thumping. My stomach hurt. I broke the silence.

"There's nothing left to work on. I want a divorce."

He brushed it off, laughing nervously. *"We're fine."*

My eyes pooled, *"No, we're not. It's over."*

His shoulders slumped over, and he cried.

It was terrible. I felt terrible. I was choosing this. I am terrible.

Shaking again, I steadied myself on the table to avoid collapsing. And then I walked home. At the empty park, October of 2008, I quit my marriage and reclaimed the courage I had lost at the marriage altar.

3. Downsizing Secrets

The next few days were a blur of revealing what I had worked so damn hard to keep hidden. My family had no idea. My dad embraced me and told me he was sorry. My mom comforted me and told me I made the right decision. She was glad I left, and it was all going to be okay.

Nevertheless, I didn't tell anyone else because I dreaded other people's reactions. Looks of pity. Their judgment. I felt such an immense shame around the whole thing — the "D" word. Practically speaking, I know you can't change someone who doesn't want to change, but the voices of doubt crept in that I didn't do enough, that I should have tried harder, that I wasn't honoring the vows I took. In sickness and health. Was abuse a sickness?

All my doubt broke when I stepped into my next counseling session. It had been one week since I asked for a divorce. All alone, I sat on the faded, rose-colored loveseat and hugged the worn throw pillow. I gave Tom the news, and he sighed compassionately.

"Let me show you something. The results are back from the marriage test you and Trevor took."

It was the kind of test that gets sifted through a big machine to measure scores based on our answers. I looked it over. We had low scores of 10-20% in nearly every category. But the piece that left me rattled was the three sentences at the bottom.

"This marriage is in crisis. There is little the couple agree on and are probably considering divorce. Monitor for an abusive situation."

Goosebumps traveled up my arms, and tears ran down my face faster than I could brush them off. Tom was silent for a moment, as it settled in my heart. I had made the right choice by quitting my marriage. Despite the advice from the church. Despite the church ignoring abuse. It was there. Even a machine could see it.

It was time to face the music and explain to the rest of my family the secret I was keeping. I was pretty confident I had done a decent job hiding all my marriage angst. Nobody would see this coming. I started with my sister. She consoled me and offered her support. Only four more siblings to tell. I was weak. I said as little as possible. But my mom believed I could use the support, and while visiting with one of my siblings, she urged me to open up a little more. I half-explained, fumbling for words, because where do you start? I managed to get out a few things, just a tiny slice of what had been, but at the end of my words, they stared at me and matter-of-factly said, "Wow, Ang, you need to grow a backbone."

At the time, I felt this as judgment, and it was followed with well-meaning advice. Such as, "Why would you stay?" and "Have you no self-respect?" and "I would have never stayed." It hurt. But now I understand. We take the things others tell us and process them through the lens of our own lives. We are walking mirrors. We see

34

and hear the difficult things others are experiencing, and we compare it to our situation. We need to know how their position correlates to our lives, if we are ahead or behind, if we are better or worse off. If we are better, we get the dopamine rush of slight superiority. If we are worse, jealousy taps on our not-enoughness. We tell ourselves we'd never be in that position. We listen and selfishly, we think about what it says about them and us. I can't explain this. I think it's biological. But we all do this to an extent. It's not fair or right, but it's how most of us are programmed to receive people's stories.

Since I couldn't see this, I shut down. I stopped discussing it. I couldn't physically do it again. I drafted a short email to my mom's sisters. "I need to let you know Trevor and I are getting a divorce. I'm not ready to talk about it. I love you all." I knew they would spread the word to my big family, so I didn't have to. And my mom and aunties, who have witnessed, experienced, and survived tough things, united around me with the love and depth of their years. A sentiment I won't forget because, between my mom and my aunties, they have seen it all. I didn't need to explain anything. Life has knocked them down a few times too. Maybe not in the same way but enough not be shaken by anything I could tell them.

Thanksgiving was rounding the corner. The energy I held to abandon my marriage ceased to exist. Like a once esteemed porcelain teacup falling on hard tile, I was shattered. I plunged myself into pajamas, slithered into my bed, and mentally checked out of life. I stayed there for two weeks, appearing only for ice cream and to check the mailbox for Netflix envelopes with season three of Desperate Housewives. I sobbed. A lot. Enough tears to overflow the dozens of empty ice cream containers I was racking up. Finally, my mom had seen plenty of loathing for one woman's divorce binge.

She walked into my room loudly announcing, "Enough. Get up. You can't do this forever. And please, take a shower."

So I did.

A few of my friends had gone through a divorce too. They got it. No explanation needed. But some of my friends didn't understand; mostly my Christian friends. There were stares of pity and disappointment. After I filed for divorce, whispers rolled about because I didn't have "Biblical grounds" to leave the marriage and people who spoke loudly in the name of Christianity, used the Bible to defend their personal views about not believing in divorce.

I heard scriptures delivered in a tone I sensed wasn't Godly, but I didn't know what to think anymore. Some said I needed to try harder. At this point, I had only opened up about the verbal abuse. Maybe I should mention the other women? Divorce for adultery was biblical, right? But what did it matter? If God required me to stay, well then, I was quite fine being disobedient because staying was hell. A burning I couldn't endure anymore.

I internalized the hurtful stuff way more than I should have. I clung tightly to my friends, who gathered around me with understanding instead of pity. And when Trevor showed up at my work to return divorce paperwork, seemingly seconds after we separated, and with a brand-new girlfriend perched in the passenger seat of my old car, my friends called him an asshole and took me to dinner.

At coffee with an old friend, she assured me I was covered because the Bible says it is okay to leave a marriage for three reasons: abuse, addiction, and adultery. Excellent, I thought. I'm covered, like auto insurance. I felt broken. Defective. Unreturnable. I tried to reconcile that the people offering me biblical advice were broken people too, and I should try to be more forgiving. It's just really hard when they are so confident in quoting scripture and being judgemental and seeking to be good accountability partners.

The damage was done. In the aftermath of divorce, I quit my theology. My fundamentals and my religious foundation were smashed to bits. For the first time in my life, I began to search for God recklessly. And myself. I say recklessly because, most of the time, it's been clumsy and needy and undignified amidst tiny moments of grace and love and liberation. But all of it involved quitting things over and over. Letting go of the things no longer required. Clinging, white-knuckled to the only thing I had: hope for something better.

4. Quitting a Hurting Season

My very first job at 16 years old was as a hostess for a Mexican restaurant. I wore a bright teal off-the-shoulder blouse, tucked into a flowing skirt, made from enough fabric to shelter a small village. At the end of a shift, my clothes smelled of stale tortilla chips and refried beans. I would come home from work, and my mom, who has the nose of a bloodhound, forced me to change in the garage because it was *that* bad.

At 17 years old, my next job was in customer service at Berean, a local Christian bookstore. I worked there on September 11, 2001, and remember it like it was yesterday. I got to work an hour after the second Twin Towers collapsed. The building smelled of its usual paperback books, strong black coffee, and Otis Spunkmeyer cookies, but it was oddly quiet. My coworkers and I shuffled silently in front of the television. It was a national tragedy, so grim management considered closing the store for the day. They ultimately decided to stay open in case people needed spiritual support. And they did.

Many customers, trying to make sense of what was happening, came in to purchase Bibles, devotionals, and books on grief. There was an equally steady stream of bizarre people I would classify in the "preppers" category, the kind who are rumored to have secret underground bunkers filled with canned green beans, stacks of ammunition, and old McDonald's ketchup packets. On this day, the preppers bought up all the books on the end times, Revelations, and a popular fiction series about the rapture, *Left Behind*. I couldn't bring myself to read the *Left Behind* series because the whole idea of the end times scared the hell out of me. It was supposed to be something we Christians believed was coming any day now. If you grew up in the Christian subculture you could probably sing along with the Crystal Lewis song about the second coming of Christ, *People Get Ready*.

I helped a woman wearing a prairie dress a few sizes too big. It draped her small body. She had large gray eyes and a matching braid that hung down her arched back, and she pointed her witchy finger at me.

Her scratchy voice reputed, "Have you heard the government is inserting people with identification cards? Mark of the Beast, I tell you. The end times are here."

"Like microchips? My dog has one. Is that what you mean?"

She sidestepped away from me like I had Ebola. "You did what?" she yelled.

I waited for a poisonous red apple to fall from her long dress. Adding the label "Christian" in front of "bookstore" brought in all kinds.

The kooks were mostly the exception. I love reading, and so walking book aisles every day was my idea of heaven. My head was endlessly in a different book. It was the time of Lee Strobel, Josh McDowell, and airy-fairy Bruce Wilkinson. We had the stern John McAurther and money collecting, Benny Hinn. We had Joyce Meyer and T.D. Jakes before he was on Oprah. Everyone had opinions on who had the right theology and who was a heretic. People would warn: be careful with this, be wary with that, be cautious with that

T.D. Jakes man, "I don't think he believes in the Trinity." Some would go off on a diatribe on the evils of *Harry Potter* or *Lord of the Rings*. There was always something to be warned about and always something to fear.

At this time, the Columbine High School shooting had happened only a few years before. It was a tragedy where several people lost their lives, including two girls singled out because of their Christian beliefs. The book, *Jesus Freaks,* was written by D.C. Talk as a reminder to the church youth that people are still losing their lives defending their faith. It was also the generation where many theology and apologetics books encouraged you to be totally sure about God and ready to answer when someone asks you about your faith. Defend your faith. Preserve. Uphold. Fight for Jesus.

I often thought of the Columbine girl who died after being asked if she was a Christian. She responded yes, and then she was shot. Would I have the guts to say yes? Would I want to say yes? I don't think so. My heart filled with guilt for feeling these cowardly things, because it must mean I'm not faithful enough. Is it wrong that I wonder what would have happened if she had said no and the shooter let her live? Would God have been mad that she denied him? Would he unsave her? Revoke her salvation? I was taught those who denied God would be denied.

When I turned 18, I left the bookstore job to sign on with the local police department as a 911 operator. Late on a graveyard shift, the phone rang.

"911, what's your emergency?"

A sweet little boy voice, maybe five years old, said, "Hello? It's Jacob."

"Are your parents there?" In my head, I could picture his little hand holding the phone.

He stuttered, "My mom is sleeping, and I can't wake her up."

The pit of my stomach dropped, remembering another call from last week that started the same way but ended in utter devastation and a few white body bags.

"Jacob, is anyone else home with you?"

"My sister, but she won't wake up either."

The pit grew deeper. "Okay, Jacob, I need you to try to wake her up. Did you try shaking her arm?"

He left the phone and a minute later came back. "I tried really, really hard, but she won't wake up."

"That's okay, honey. Police officers are going to help you. Okay?" I chatted with him for a few minutes while alternating clicking my pen with drumming my fingers on the desk. Click. Drum. Click. Drum. Every second felt like an hour. Finally, the officers arrived on the scene. I told Jacob to set the phone down and open the door to let in the officers. The phone line was still open. I heard the officers enter. I sat at my desk miles away, praying for the sake of this little boy, his mom and sister were okay.

I could hear the officers announcing their presence and then marching down the hall to the mom's bedroom. And then I hear a mom screech. Clearly alive and clearly upset that she awoke to two large police officers in her bedroom standing over her.

"What the hell is going on?" She screamed.

She pulled herself together, as the officers explained Jacob's call. A poor, sleep-deprived mother. Jacob had called just for the fun of it. I'm sure he was in for a scolding, but I was glad they were okay. In the dispatcher room, we had a little laugh and went back to work. Two nights later, Jacob called, and as it would happen, the call came in my line again. This time he was upfront that he wanted to shoot the breeze. I had made a new friend. Maybe a few years later now, it's a story his mother tells with a smile on her face. Maybe.

The dispatch job was a grownup job with a grownup paycheck, and I started looking for my own place. It was 2003 in Southern California, and new buildings and hurried homes rose from the ground like spring mushrooms. My mom and I toured a brand new, beautiful apartment complex. We ooh-ed and ahhhh-ed over the white crown molding and the smell of newly unrolled, upgraded carpet. My mom likely knew I couldn't afford this, but not before I fell in love with a two-bedroom, two-bath floor plan with a wrap-around countertop in the kitchen and large patio overlooking a lush tree line. I mentally moved my furniture in and dreamed of all of the fancy dinner parties with my friends, and the Jane Austin books I'd read at dusk on the patio. When the leasing agent revealed the cost, I knew it was a hard no. Even if I had attempted to survive on beans and rice, my grownup paycheck still wasn't enough. I sadly let go of this dream.

Fast-forward to life after I filed for divorce. It was 2008, the economy had gone belly up, and all those beautiful new homes that had sprung up sat empty. People were losing their jobs, cashing out their 401Ks, and gleaning TV shows about couponing. It was all about survival. Many people began to question the American dream.

I had a thriving event planning business and had done exceptionally well the last few years but now was suffering. I was lucky enough to get a receptionist job at the church I was attending, and I enrolled in college full-time. Again. I was thankful to be living with my parents, but I needed my own space.

I started looking at renting a room. Houses were foreclosing at record speed, and everyone was looking to lease, driving up the cost of rentals. Finding a roommate was my only option. On a too hot and sticky Monday morning in May, a man who attended the church walked into the office and asked if I knew anyone looking for an apartment.

"Oh, yes, me."

Until he told me the lofty price.

"Oh. Not me. But I'd be happy to spread the word for you."

The man, Mark, jotted his information on a post-it note and left.

The next day I was complaining to my coworkers, Julie, Gina, and Stephanie, about not finding a room to rent that wasn't roach-infested on the scary side of town when Mark returned. He explained how yesterday, as he drove by the church, he'd felt an uncanny nudge to stop in the office to ask about his apartment. He believed the tug of the situation too exceptional to be anything but led by God.

"I'd like you to rent my apartment. I know you can't afford it, but we'll make it work for you."

Sensing it'd be a deal-breaker, I confessed, "I have two big dogs."

"No worries," he assured. "The complex allows large breeds. Actually, the unit is right by the dog run. I'll tell you what, meet my wife and me this afternoon, and we can talk about rent."

"Well, okay, then." Wow, my own space. My heart jumped, and I told it to calm down.

I knew it was too good to be true, but he scribbled the address down, and a few hours later, I drove to the apartment.

As I pulled my car into the apartment parking lot, I was altogether speechless, which my friends would assure you is an anomaly. But as I walked up to the exact same apartment I toured with my mom seven years before, with the exact same lovely, white crown molding and the patio overlooking the trees, my mouth hung open like a fish on a hook. I knew it was a dream, and someone would be waking me up any second. I met Mark and his wife, Nancy, at the front, and we walked inside.

Inside he spoke up, "The apartment is yours until December 31. We've prayed about it, and we both were thinking of pricing rent at $500 for you." Less than a third of the price he'd mentioned the day before.

Nancy said, "It was kinda random. My mom, before we told her, she unknowingly also suggested $500. Will that work for you?"

I wildly nodded before considering any details. I'd make it work. If I had to sell my plasma, I would. First, I'd have to figure out what plasma is, but it was just a detail at this point. Plus, it was cheaper than any roommate situation I had found. They gave me the keys and the mailbox code and explained the well-loved, hunter green leather couches would have to stay in the apartment, but I could have them. I was beside myself with the magic unfolding. I said yes, and thank you. Even though we attended the same church, I had never met Mark and Nancy before. We were still strangers as they handed me the keys. I remained awe-struck over how they would gift me this and danced home to tell my parents. I had never known a stranger to take such a chance on me with so few questions, and at the exact moment I needed it.

Back at my parent's house, I needed to scrounge up the money for the first month's rent. I looked for my checkbook. It was always in the same place, and now when I needed it most, it was missing. Of course. I spent an hour tearing my bedroom to shreds trying to find it. Finally, in the last place left to look, I opened a small drawer and pushed aside old swimsuits in three different sizes that I was holding out hope that one day - *one day* - my body would shrink enough for them to fit. But it was highly unlikely because they had sat in the drawer for so long, I'm sure the moment I tried to stretch one over my hiney, the brittle elastic would crumble like a day-old muffin. But hidden under the swimsuits was a black leather journal. I picked it up and out fell a white bank envelope. Immediately I flashed back to a cash tip I received from a wedding client. How could I forget about this? I opened the envelope and poured out the contents. My hands shook as I counted five $100 bills.

I spent the next six months in the crown molding apartment, on the back patio overlooking the lush trees. Reading books and praying and healing and learning how to dream new dreams. I've heard about miracles, like Jesus turning water into wine or toddlers who sleep through the night. Maybe this doesn't rightly meet the miracle criteria, yet I wholeheartedly believe the apartment was a gift from God. A white flag of restoration for my broken heart.

5. Downsizing Books

In the sixth grade, I joined the Missionettes Girls Club, the church's equivalent to Girl Scouts, complete with a vest and camping badges. On a summer camping trip, the leaders announced a contest for the girl who could display the most amount of Ruth-like character and the unfading beauty of a gentle and quiet spirit. We were taught to be gentle and quiet is of great worth to God. The grand prize was trifold: a gift card, the most adorable stuffed animal puppy, and an official-looking Ruth Attitude Certificate. I wanted to win so badly, I could taste it, but a gentle and quiet spirit, I had not. If they had a certificate for being loud, and plump with a quirky laugh, I'd win for sure. But I still tried my best. All weekend, I helped. I volunteered for meal prep and chores. I prayed awkwardly out loud, and I handed out compliments like Oprah gives out cars. Not one word of gossip came from my mouth. Nor did I tell anyone it was, in fact, Misty who clogged the toilet so that I wouldn't embarrass her. How nice of me. At lunch, I sat by the girl who had no friends, and for two days, tried my damnedest to live like Jesus. And it must have worked because at the end of the week, I was crowned with the Ruth award. When I got back home, I pushed the certificate on my wall with a bent thumbtack, and within a day, I was back to acting like a normal person because wearing a gentle and quiet spirit all the time is like wearing faux leather pants. It's okay for a few hours, but after that, it's sweaty and unnatural, and you'll get a yeast infection.

My parents sent me to a Christian high school. I had heard rumors about rebellious private school kids and crazy Catholic girls. Unlike most religious schools I knew about, these kids were actually into Jesus. They wore WWJD bracelets, asked how "my walk" was, and perfected the appropriate male/female side hug. Wednesday was chapel day, and at lunchtime, a group of Ruth-like girls would sit under an oak tree for bible study, and talk about what it meant to follow Jesus. We would shuffle our Bibles open as wet grass seeped from the blanket to our jeans. The leader, a high school junior, was everything the Ruth award was about. She prayed, with a low, soft voice, solemn and dignified with the most skilled, godly religious words. She went around the circle and collected prayer requests. Praying out loud terrified me. I'd give my "unspoken" request followed by half a dozen other unspokens, and there was always that one girl, a hot mess, who would overshare her insecurities of broken friendships, boy troubles, and her parents impending divorce. Looking back, I wish I was more like her. As we all tried to hide our fears, she bravely owned hers.

We read *I Kissed Dating Goodbye*, the most popular Christian book on dating in 2000. It preached traditional dating is "a training ground for divorce."[1] It suggested old-fashioned alternatives like courting in groups and not kissing until the marriage altar. Everyone was reading it. Like a rite of passage, your parents would buy you a silver purity ring, the one with a heart, lock, and key, and this book. It was a best-selling paperback chock-full of things Jesus didn't mention about dating, bless His forgetful heart. This book is the Christian travel agency of guilt trips, teaching that with every person you date, you give them a piece of your heart and you will never, ever get it back. By the time you make it to your wedding, all washed up, you'll have only half a heart to give to your spouse. And to bring this all home, it provides an illustration of a man and woman standing at the altar, ready to say vows but then all the groom's ex-girlfriends walk up grabbing his other hand. He tells his wife, he's sorry, but she can only have what's left of his heart. Lovely.

Some have said the damage done by this book has led to higher divorce rates for my millennial, church-going demographic, and I don't think it's a far stretch. This book was groundbreaking during my high school years. It served as a gateway for teens to marry too early because, well, hormones and purity, and also for couples to stay in bad marriages because who is going to want washed up divorcees with only half a heart to give. It sounded a lot like my first marriage. And about half a dozen of my friend's relationships. While the brokenhearted and companionless part of me wants to blame Joshua Harris for the toxic book, I can't blame him entirely for the casualties of his book, because as I'm sitting in church, newly divorced and listening to a marriage retreat announcement, I can't help but wonder where the church's leadership and accountability was during all of this dating book nonsense? Harris was 21 when he wrote it. He couldn't rent an Enterprise Rent-A-Car. He was barely legal to order a Jello shot. Which we know he probably didn't do because he was busy writing the book. And can we even trust someone who has never had a Jello shot? I don't think so. *Twenty-one.* Leadership in the Christian church, ignoring all red flags blazing, promoted his dating message, and the flawed advice made it to the bookshelves of more than a million teens.

Our churches want to promote abstinence, which isn't a bad thing, but in the process have we considered how dangerous it is to use shaming methods and severely limiting or altogether leaving out vital information on safe sex, birth control, and sexually transmitted diseases because kids should just say no to the horizontal tango? I've heard so many stories of pastors comparing those who are doing the deed outside of marriage to nasty chewed up gum, used toothbrushes, and a thorny rose stripped of its petals. One time I saw a church leader, in an attempt to promote abstinence, put a piece of Duct Tape on his arm.

"This represents how sex bonds us in a relationship," he explained. Then he pulled the tape up and put it on someone else's arm, noting it was less sticky. He pulled the tape off and put it on a third arm. "See how the glue is gone? By the time you get married, you will have little bond left if you're intimate before marriage."

Used Duct Tape? Is this the best we can do? Where is the redemption of Jesus? Where is a message of hope and restoration? Is God even in the restoration business?

Divorced. Broken. I desperately needed the restoration God promised. I recently heard a pastor say God restores us to our pristine condition with a picture of an old, damaged Cadillac junker, restored to a perfectly shiny, new Cadillac. While I get the sentiment, most of the time, I feel like an old, dented Camry with alignment problems. Saying God will restore us to new is a dangerous message because it assumes a few things. Like the dents we've endured need to be polished away as if they never happened. This kind of restoration makes me feel like I have to renounce my low points and that I was perfect, or should have been before they happened. The truth is I was naive before, and hard knocks showed me genuine empathy, love, and God.

Second, it diminishes God to a magician holding a glitter wand, "Just believe...abracadabra!!" And BAM, you'll feel whole, healed, and normal. Belief in that kind of restoration is risky because it plays our emotions, creating an overload of spiritual high and inevitably a crash when we don't feel 100% like new. Perhaps it's more correct to say we're recycled again and again - transformed into something new and usable - rather than restored to our former selves. I will forever be a hot mess. Restoration doesn't mean looking perfect, and it's not a quick fix to our health, finances, or anxiety. Restoration is something that happens to our souls and renews the hope things can be better. It's a peace about our existence and freedom from failures and heartache.

In an oddly paradoxical story of restoration, Joshua Harris spoke at TED in November 2017. In his talk, he told the audience how he had discovered the transformational power in admitting when we are wrong and that he was, in fact, fundamentally wrong about many things in his book. He said the fame of the book made it easy to write off the critics as haters. To hide behind the ones who praised his writing. For him, admitting he was wrong was challenging because it felt like he would be saying a big part of his life was wrong. He has received a lot of pushback on his new stance, both from the people whom his book hurt and the ones who loved it.

> "I'm learning that admitting you're wrong will tick some people off…possibly because if you admit you're wrong and they [had] agreed with you then, by implication, they are wrong. And they don't want to deal with that. So they'd rather you stay the way you are, then have to face up to that themselves." Harris said.

Some are questioning his motivation for coming forward. I'm not sure what I think yet, but I admire his courage to apologize.

Restoration is the opportunity to rebuild: our finances, our relationships, our family patterns, and our beliefs. It's opening up the rusty hood with a trusted mechanic and getting to work. Rebuilding is a dirty process and takes tools of courage and sweat and many, many hours laboring over a hot engine where we'll likely get burned in the process. Restoration won't change your past, but it will make it mean something. It's hard work. It's uncomfortable. It's not pretty. But the goal is to rebuild and restore a more truthful self-image, esteemed in hope and love. This restoration is what I needed.

6. The Courage to Start Over

My time at the crown molding apartment was up. It hurt saying goodbye to my sacred space. On January 1, 2010, I collected enough empty boxes behind the local grocery store to pack everything and moved to the Point Loma neighborhood in San Diego. Friends helped me unload dozens of boxes - now stacked to the ceiling in the tiny 600 square foot beach apartment. With lots of unpacking to do, I grabbed my keys and pups and headed straight to the beach.

My life now included at least one trip a day to see the ocean in all its glory. My German shepherd, Giada, would run in the waves. My golden retriever, Apple, would chase tennis balls, even the ones tossed for other dogs. It's how I made friends on the beach. The water was so spectacular and healing. I would find a place to sink in the sand and watch the waves turn for hours. We would stay as long as possible before I loaded the dogs and, unintentionally, gallons upon gallons of sand back into my silver Eclipse and head home. I could vacuum for an entire year and still make a sandcastle from what's left. Seven years after I moved, I still had pieces of San Diego sand following me around. The sand is untamable. The variety of sand reminds me of all the people who come into our lives. Some sand is silky, warm, and welcoming. Other sand is more like worn gravel, you bear the dust and annoyance but only because you get to see the ocean. And other times sand is more like sharp rocks; so painful and sometimes dangerous, you'll need a barrier to walk it safely.

If sand is like people, then God must be the Ocean. Sometimes graceful. Sometimes fierce. Sand attaches to us like sea sludge, and the Ocean, big and powerful, washes it all away. For a second. But there's more sand. And then a wave. More sand. Another wave. It's a forever dance of tenderness, love, and renewal. The Ocean's current never stops guiding the sand, molding and sculpting it into priceless seascapes. Maybe the truth is, you can't reach the Ocean without walking through the sand. It is the gateway to feel, see, and touch the All-Powerful Ocean.

After pouring my heart out to the Ocean, I would head back to my over-embellished apartment, filled with things I collected since my divorce. A tiger-oak, pedestal kitchen table. A vintage dresser I practically stole off craigslist. The softest, 600 thread count king sheets, in a deep eggplant shade, that I put on my credit card as a housewarming gift to myself. Even the worn green leather couches, the ones the couple gave me when I left the crown-molding apartment, felt entirely at home. It was wonderful and cozy and even more perfect because it was all mine. I didn't need anyone's permission to hang a picture or tell me how to arrange the furniture. This space was a banner for the person I was becoming.

A small police department in San Diego County hired me as an emergency operator. Although not my passion, it was familiar and a stable paycheck during a down-turned economy. I needed a break from wedding planning and happiness and gagging when I'd see lovey-dovey couples. I wasn't bitter. Clearly.

I spent my days studying police codes and working too many 12-hour shifts. Answering 911 calls is nothing like I imagined. You'd think it would be helping people perform CPR and talking dads-to-be through delivering their very own babies over the phone because they were too far from the hospital, and the baby was crowning. But it's mostly a lot of dysfunctional people bothered by their neighbor's loud music and fender benders and city officials calling to demand their election opponent's ads be removed from people's lawns because *"Do You Know Who I Am?"*

A 75-year-old woman called and wanted me to send an officer to arrest the 74-year-old man who, she said, tricked her into sleeping with him, as they do.

"He told me he was deploying to Iraq, and I felt bad for him."

I found myself giving an elderly woman sex advice.

"I'm sorry, ma'am. Sometimes men lie. You have to be careful who you sleep with."

At least you didn't marry him, I thought.

I was making pennies, and the job was relentless and all-consuming, but even though my bank account was as empty as Jesus's tomb, my soul was full. I made new friends. I was head over heels in love with San Diego. And by spending my days jogging at the beach, I dropped nearly fifty pounds of stress weight from the last few years. I was developing a new normal, whatever normal is, and I was starting to feel something I forgot existed - happiness.

I began opening to the idea of falling in love again. People talk about the so-called fish in the pond, but when I tried dating before I moved to San Diego, the pond was chock-full of clownfish. Jobless. Married. Or peculiar, and not in the right way. Like every newly divorced millennial, I tried online dating but made the mistake of starting with the free dating website, Plenty of Fish. The first date was coffee with a guy named Joe, whom I thought was a tad overdressed for Frappuccinos in a full black suit and tie. He was nervous and chatty and profusely sweating because it was a summer evening and still 90 degrees outside. I discovered he loved polar bears, to the point of obsession. I thought it was sweet as he handed me a stuffed polar bear toy for my dogs, but then I noticed he was wearing a polar bear tie. And hat. And I spent the next 30 minutes trying to pretend I wasn't weirded out by all of this as he showed me dozens of photos on his cellphone of his white bear collection. I went on three more dates with different prospects, which all equated to a circus side-show act, and decided maybe I'm not ready for this dating charade.

But I had come a long way in San Diego and since the polar bear guy. My bitterness from divorce was subsiding, and I started to crave romance and long walks on the beach and someone else to kill the occasional bug in my apartment. I wanted a best friend and a whirlwind love story. Basically, I wanted *The Notebook,* and ultimately a few babies. All of it. Was it too much to ask? I hoped not.

Driving home from the police department, I listened to Leann Rimes belt out her song, *Something's Gotta Give*, about a thirty-one-year old gal who thought she'd be in love, married, and driving a minivan by now. I asked the Power Who Is, *if you're not too busy, I think I'm ready. Could you send me someone who doesn't smoke, who will be careful with my bruised heart, and who's a decent blend of funny and smart? And also, God, you remember I have a thing for redheads, right?*

To help tip things in my favor, and in case God was too busy, I joined eHarmony. It was in the early days of online dating when you were no longer meeting people at a bar, but way before swiping left and right was a thing, and you had to virtually wave or poke or high-five people. In the first week, two guys "waved" at me, and a few days later, I headed out to meet one at a Mexican restaurant. I was on my way to my own Noah and Allie story, and when we each ordered the same taco combination plate, I heard,"If you're a bird, then I'm a bird." The conversation was easy, and while there were no considerable flying sparks, there was no mention of polar bears. He was sweet and caring, but he sealed his fate when he barely touched his plate before announcing he was full. Call it insecurity or shallowness, maybe somewhere in the middle, but I can't date someone who eats less than me at dinner. It's not just because I've heard rumors that people who enjoy food are better in bed, but because I'm Mexican and Irish, and the women in my family feed their husbands like it's a religion. But also, the bed thing. I let him go.

The second guy, a nonsmoking Christian, seemed to have the perfect mix of humor and cynicism in our email correspondence. His name was Jeff, and he had a job in the Coast Guard. He also had red hair, which he tried calling strawberry blond, but he was unmistakably ginger.

For a few weeks, we messaged back and forth. Until one chilly evening, I found myself driving to a tiny wine bar in the corner of San Diego. He was waiting for me at a table on the patio, just past the fire pit. Our eyes locked, and I melted a little. A glass or two of Pinot Noir later, I had collected some information about him.

He was from Orange County, California and went to college in Connecticut before landing back in San Diego. I asked too many questions because a side effect of working at the police department left me thinking everyone using online dating services was a potential ax murderer. Upon arrival, I had texted his name and vehicle license plate to my best friend, Stefanie. She knows the drill. I would call her in about two hours. If I didn't call, she would send a search party. He seemed safe enough, but I dodged the question about where I lived by giving the general neighborhood then changed the subject.

The evening grew chilly, and we moved closer to the fire pit so we wouldn't have to leave. We took the hint when our waiter pretended to check on us for the third time after the staff started pulling the chairs inside for closing. Jeff walked me to my car and gave me a polite hug goodbye. With a little tug on my heart, I could see our second date. I started my engine and called Stefanie to tell her how my date went, and in my rear-view window, I noticed his black Jeep close behind my car. Another mile and he was still behind me.

Another mile and I told Stefanie, "I think he's following me."

"Oh, my God! What are you going to do?"

"I don't know. I could drive to the police station, but I'm already by my apartment."

I made a turn. He made the same turn.

"Just my luck. I met a stalker." I assert.

Was he going to snatch me? Just my luck. I would be kidnapped and spend the next year in a damp basement handcuffed to some old rickety desk, and he would slide trays of cold oatmeal under the door for me. Breakfast, lunch, and dinner, all cold oatmeal. Because mushy oatmeal is the scientific, authoritarian food of torture. Maybe I would convince him to let me listen to the radio, teach myself Morse code, and send covert messages to a search team. This would ensure my rescue. The Today show would report it, and, naturally, Katie Couric would do the interview. Was that a car honk? I zoned back in.

Just as Stefanie and I were drafting my escape from the inevitable kidnapping unfolding, Jeff called me. I put Stefanie on hold and clicked over.

"I don't want you to think I'm following you. I live in this neighborhood."

I stayed breezy and silently promised myself to stop watching Dateline.

"What? I'd never think that."

It so happens, out of 1.4 million people in San Diego, our buildings were right next door to each other. Next. Door. Not bad, eHarmony. Not bad.

7. Rightsizing Love

An officer at the police department had asked me out a few times - just as friends, of course, because he was married. He wanted to take me on a motorcycle ride.

"Never. No way I'm getting on that death trap. I'm not a stunt woman."

It wasn't the fast motorcycle I was avoiding, but the brazen married guy trying to be friendly and I was too much of a weenie to call him out.

A few days after the wine bar date, I did find myself on the back seat of a blue motorcycle, my arms wrapped around Jeff, the redhead. I hugged his waist as we flew up Interstate 8 to the little Danish town of Julian, just outside the city. It was our second date, and I splurged on a faux leather jacket from Nordstrom's Rack because leather is pretty much required for motorcycle riding. Oh, and cute, pink ballet shoes.

When Jeff picked me up for the date he looked down at my shoes, and his eyebrow went up. "You look cute, but you can't wear those shoes."

"What do you mean I can't wear these shoes?"

I didn't mention I bought them specifically for our date.

"They aren't safe for a motorcycle. Don't you have tennis shoes?"

"Well, yes, but I don't wear tennis shoes with jeans."

I'm no Rachel Zoe, but certain lines need to be drawn. For example, grown adults who wear overalls, popped collars, crocs, or jeans embellished with studded crosses. No. Wrong. Stop. I think we all have some fashion faux pas we can't avoid. Despite my better judgment, I will forever love entire monochromatic velour tracksuits in bright funky colors, preferably with something agreeable written over the tush. Can we ask Miranda Priestly to bring those back? And scrunchies. But on that day, I succumb to the sneakers and jeans mostly because I didn't want Jeff to think I was high maintenance this early in the dating game. And because I'm not high maintenance, generally speaking. The night ended with our first kiss despite my fashion horror. So there's that.

Now I consider myself a feminist, and I believe women can do anything a man can do, but I also believe in chivalry. I know, I'm a walking contradiction. But what woman isn't? That's probably not very feminist of me, but I do my best to hold the tension. Anyway, while I have no problem paying for dates, I think the first date should be paid for by the guy. After that, it's fair game. On our first date at the wine bar, when the bill came, I did the pretend to grab for my purse.

Jeff said, "Oh no, I'll get it this time."

And the second time we went out I offered to pay. The third time he paid. So on our fourth date, Jeff suggested the Cheesecake Factory. Which is fine, except in the date-paying-rotation, it was my turn, and the Cheesecake Factory isn't cheap. Add in drinks and a tip, and I was in big trouble because I didn't have two dimes to rub together. I knew by the time we finished, I would have to excuse myself to the back kitchen and wash dishes. The waiter dropped the check into the middle of the table, and Jeff quickly grabbed it, and I narrowly missed a potentially awkward situation.

My car payment leftover from the divorce was astronomical, and all four tires were Dwayne Johnson bald. My salary at the police department was meager. I was paid twice a month, and often after bills, I'd have a scanty $25 to my name until the next payday. After a careful calculation of the distance to work and miles per gallon, I'd put $5 in the tank. $15 went for groceries. I learned a bag of apples, a loaf of bread, and a jar of peanut butter can go a long way. Finally, $5 for a Venti Iced Americano, because I deserved it. I was a working girl and damn proud of it. I was making it on my own, but just barely, and I didn't want to be in the Cheesecake Factory tangle again. I needed to make some money.

Enter my new Craigslist business. I listed my George Foreman, my waffle iron, and a few other small appliances I had left from my first marriage. One night when Jeff came to pick me up, he questioned the mountain of small gadgets on my kitchen table.

I glanced over the remnants of a life I no longer lived.

I made nonchalant hand flutters. "I'm selling them."

"Why would you sell your waffle maker?" Jeff gasped. "I love waffles."

"Me too." I grabbed my purse. "But I just wanted a little extra cash this week."

I didn't make a big deal about it and never expected or asked, but he picked up the tab that night. I didn't mind being broke because I had the beach, which was always free and within walking distance. Even more valuable, I had a viable amount of self-respect developing in the places bankrupted by my first marriage. And I think being penniless, while paying your rent and making it on your own, should be a rite of passage for women before they consider marriage. To know that I could, and have, made it on my own is an enormously freeing.

My job was going well. I started work at 5:30 am, an ungodly hour, but still magnificent in San Diego. One dreary Wednesday, I was particularly happy to wake at the wee hours because it was my work "Friday." Even more, I had a date with Jeff that evening, a man who was stealing my heart one motorcycle ride at a time. So, at 4:00 am, I stumbled around, pulled a sweatshirt over my tank top, and leashed my pups for their morning walk. I usually have a good grip, but that morning, they seemed to be dragging me to the sandbox. It was a volleyball court converted into a dog run, and this is where morning business happened. It was still way too early for the sun and besides a tiny street light in the distance, it was pitch black. I let them off leash and waited. I danced around in my shorts, trying to warm up. Maybe I should have put on pants. No sooner than they ran off, my German Shepherd raced back to me whimpering. She was sneezing and rubbing her nose on me, getting dog snot all over my bare leg. I couldn't figure out what her fuss was until I got a whiff of it. It wasn't dog snot. It was skunk.

She'd been sprayed and was trying to sponge it off of her face. Onto my leg. The stench accelerated as I sprinted back to my apartment, wishing I had a better-enclosed patio to put her in. In calm-freakout-mode and with one hand grasping her collar, trying to hold her a steady distance from my furniture, I opened my laptop and Googled, *dog sprayed with skunk what to do*. The clock was biting at me because, as a police operator, the job is paramilitary and rigid, and there was zero wiggle room for tardiness. One gal had just been fired for being late.

Google offered up two suggestions. A recipe of dishwashing soap and hydrogen peroxide, and tomato sauce. I had neither and made aim for the grocery store. I didn't want to leave the dog in my apartment because I feared she'd settle on the green leather couch or worse, my bed. Decidedly, I loaded her into my car, reasoning a smelly vehicle would be better than a skunky bed. On the way, I had a flashback of a women's speaker I'd seen a year before telling a silly, yet true story of how a skunk sprayed her dog and she successfully used Summer's Eve douche to get out the foulness. At the store, I quickly gathered supplies, and just in case the lady was right, several bottles of douche and got in line.

As I waited, I became keenly aware that I was a walking hot mess. Disheveled. Bloodshot eyes with traces of yesterday's smudged mascara. Pajama bottoms. My eau de cologne la skunk. I used one hand to try to flatten my untamable hair as I pushed the hydrogen peroxide, tomato sauce, and douche onto the conveyor belt. The checker, a lanky college boy with bleach-blond streaks, gave me a horrified look as he scanned the 20 bottles of Summer's Eve douche. Like I was the crazy one. *Loser.*

Rushing home, I put the dog in the bath and poured all the shopping contents on her fur. It was now 4:45 am. Like a bat out of hell, I half-showered, jumped into my uniform, and hauled to work. I sat in my boss's office with wet hair and a faint smell of skunk while he raked me over the coals because, despite my valid attempts, I was still 30 minutes late. I muddled through my 12-hour shift and let my tears fall on the drive home. Instead of calling, I sent Jeff a text canceling our date to avoid sobbing into the phone. Once I was home, I gave my pup two more tomato and douche baths.

After several baths for the pup and me, I called Jeff to apologize for canceling. He talked me into walking to his building next door. I strolled over and stood on his doorstep, hesitating because I still smelled like a skunk. But he ignored the lingering smell and pulled me inside. He brushed his lips on the top of my head and gave me chocolate peanut butter cup frozen yogurt and rubbed my shoulders and let me vent about the skunk, my dreadful boss, and this awful, awful day. I let myself fully sink into his arms, and everything else faded away.

It was the exact moment I knew I loved him.

8. *Downsizing Limiting Beliefs*

One night, Jeff made the long drive next door to pick me up for a sushi date. As he turned the Jeep from West Point Loma Blvd. to Nimitz Blvd., Jeff was talking to me, but I was hangry and distracted by a beautiful couple standing in front of my favorite sandwich deli. They seemed to be fighting and utterly oblivious to the homeless man pushing his dog in a baby stroller trying to shuffle past them. She was pointing at herself, pounding her index finger on her chest. He threw his hands up in condescension, shouting, "Fine!" and then stormed down the street. It was all very fascinating, but I quickly zoned back to my place, sitting next to Jeff. He had just finished saying something he seemed excited about, and I had no idea what he was talking about. What had I missed? I didn't want him to think I was rude and not listening, even though that was regrettably what I had just done.

I didn't know what to say, so I said, "Wow, that's awesome."

I found out later that he had told me that he was just accepted to graduate school and was moving 2,500 miles away to Washington D.C. very soon. Facepalm.

Six weeks later, following my heart, I found myself behind the wheel of my old, silver Eclipse, driving away from the West Coast towards the nation's capital. Sure, it'd only been a few months, but I was in love and rolling the dice. I drove the entire way with my two pups. We stopped in Flagstaff and Albuquerque. Just after we passed Amarillo, I stopped to fill the tank and let my pups out. Apple thought it'd be a good time to roll in the dirt. Only it was a giant pile of horse manure. There I was at a gas station in the middle of nowhere, and my dog had an inch-thick coat of cow shit. I ignored my parent's advice of not talking to strangers and let a grisly trucker help me bathe her before putting her back in my car.

Back on the road and trying to make up for the lost time, I sped through most of Oklahoma until I got a ticket. This eventually turned into a warrant for my arrest because I was broke and didn't pay it right away, but that's a story for another day. One more night in Little Rock and another in Knoxville before I made it D.C. Head over heels in love. Adrenalized. Hopeful.

I promised myself never to get stuck in a bad relationship again, and I kept just enough money in my savings account in case I needed to leave. My logical backup plan was to move to Yellowstone and secure a job as a park ranger or maybe an equestrian tour guide. I knew this was a sensible backup plan because my girlfriend and I once took a road trip to Yellowstone, and we met a strand of people who gloriously wander from one national park to another and spend their days leading horse riding tours in the most beautiful areas. I'd ridden a horse once when I was fifteen, for an entire hour. So I'm sure I would qualify. Fingers crossed I didn't need my plan B.

Looking back, Jeff and I really didn't know each other, but we were confident enough in love to try. Still new in town, I had no job and no friends. We joined a small church group to get plugged into the community. The first meeting went like this.

"Let's go around the room. Say your name and what you do."

"I'm a computer scientist."

"I work for the F.B.I."

"I'm an intelligence researcher." (Which I'm pretty sure is code for working at the C.I.A.)

"I fly Air Force 2."

I'm not even kidding.

If you've never been to Washington, D.C., you introduce yourself by saying what your job title is. All powerful jobs. All with influence.

Mine was something like, "Ah, hi, I'm a 26-year-old divorced, unemployed, back-in-college-again-to-hopefully-finish-this-time student. Pleased to meet you all."

I nearly jumped down the fire escape after someone asked where I went to school, and I replied the name of my high school, not realizing everyone in the room had, at a minimum, a master's degree. Welcome to D.C. The hub of power and influence and now tiny, little me.

No fancy title. No power. No influence.

I got a job for a hot minute at a doctor's office. A couple owned it, and the wife was a no-frills, high energy idealist but also a bit of a bully. She was training me on calling insurance companies to check patient's coverage. While I was on hold, she would badger me.

"Are you stressed out? Is this making you nervous? Are you stressed yet?"

She'd say it with a smirk like I was a horse she was trying to break.

"Umm, no. Nope, I've answered 911 calls for actual emergencies. I think I can manage insurance reps."

I didn't mind taking instructions, but she couldn't stop nagging me or making sly remarks about my cleavage showing, a problem that wasn't going anywhere because with a G cup, I had cleavage in a turtleneck. I thought my shirts were proper enough for a church service with my grandmother, who is, in fact, quite spicy herself, so maybe not the best example. My boss was refined and pretty and had the perfect runner's body, and my girls were a problem she couldn't understand. And also, they'd let their two-year-old run the office, expecting me to watch him, but not reprimand him, as he poured containers of paper clips all over the floor I would then have to pick up. Like I said, the job lasted a hot minute.

A few months in, I fell into place. I felt at home in the studio apartment, and my relationship with Jeff was blossoming like the cherry trees around the tidal basin. We strolled around D.C. visiting the Smithsonian museums, the National Mall (which, as it turns out, isn't an actual mall), and sampling all the food during restaurant week. On weekends we would drive to Philly, Baltimore, and Annapolis. For Christmas, we took the train to New York City. There's nothing more romantic than strolling through Central Park when it's lightly snowing during the holidays. We saw a show on Broadway, made out on Top of the Rock, and shared a sugar rush via the cupcakes at Magnolia's Bakery. We were diving headfirst in love.

Back in D.C., I found the perfect job in event planning. Right up my alley. Something I could talk about. Something to say when people ask the only question they ever do ask when you live in Washington, DC, "What do you do?" Career and love. I soaked it up.

But if I learned anything in D.C. besides how to parallel park, it's that everyone becomes irrelevant, making a career a dangerous place to put your identity. Everyone is as replaceable as A.A. batteries. And not just replaceable but forgettable. There was a woman who worked her tail off for ten years, making the company millions. She sat at the same desk with a clear vintage candy dish she'd keep full of mini Snickers bars and butterscotch candies, and Tootsies Rolls nobody ever wanted until they were the only thing left. Coworkers would endlessly stop by to say hi, and to chit chat about the latest client gossip. Yet after she quit, while her office seat was still warm, management peeled her name off the door, and she became a distant memory. Perhaps placing your identity in a career is like having a pet boa constrictor your crazy Uncle Eddie swears is perfectly safe. You wear it proudly because it's somewhat glamorous and exotic until the snake goes missing, and you can't sleep at night wondering where the hell it went.

One evening, I stood greeting people as they arrived at a celebrity-packed event in D.C. I never tire of seeing movie stars in real life. Not in a star stuck, weak in the knees way, except for Stephen Colbert because I absolutely adore him, but in a "Wow, the camera *does* add five pounds" kinda way. Because as luck would have it, everyone is much skinnier in real life. Bless them.

At cocktail hour, the band played a rendition of an Aerosmith song, and I was instructed to circle the room and invite the people to take their seats for dinner. Asking celebrities to move anywhere is like herding blind cats. Most would give my attempts a gracious nod. Some were friendly but would avoid any eye contact and continuing chatting. Then there were a few, very few, who were downright gruff with their larger-than-life personalities, flawless faces and breathing their holier-than-thou air while their body language screamed, "Say one word to me, and I'll squash you like a bug."

I walked up to one of America's favorite movie mobsters, standing with his wife and another guest. I grew up watching his movies. With clammy hands, I invited them to take their seats because the first course was going to be served. And they didn't even so much as look at me. I thought maybe they didn't hear me, so I cleared my throat and repeated myself. The wife pursed her lips, conveying her disdain for me while dismissing me simultaneously. The rejection was so effortless, I was impressed. It was as if she had practiced this a dozen times, which I'm sure she had. The truth about celebrities is that they are just ordinary people, like us. Some nice. Some, not so much. And every one of them is precisely six inches shorter in person than whatever you thought they were, except for Stephen Colbert. It is science.

Later I was standing next to a man who owns a few hotels, Mr. Marriott.

"How is your evening going?"

Wait, is he talking to me?

I cleared my throat. "Wonderful. And how about yours?"

"Fantastic," he said, taking a sip of his beverage.

Then I told him I had just quoted an article he had recently published in my college paper. He seemed impressed I had read his piece and asked me about my educational goals. Hold The Phone. Mr. Marriott, the owner of six thousand hotels, asked little ole me about my goals. I was nervous and made a self-deprecating joke about being in school so long I should be a brain surgeon any day now. The music was loud, and my humor got lost in the noise. He nodded and congratulated me on becoming a doctor. With the music blaring, I didn't correct him.

Later as I thought about this, I had a realization. I've always told myself that girls like me, who take a dozen years to finish a four-year degree, don't become brain surgeons. Girls like me go to community college. Girls like me have big hair, not big dreams. But now I ask - why not me? Look at people like Chris Gardner, J.K. Rowling, and Oprah. So many people come from humble beginnings and pull themselves up to accomplish remarkable things. Why not me?

All the blessings to people who fall into our lives and unknowingly make one tiny comment that shows us how we are keeping our potential confined by our past, stifled from our family's past, or imprisoned by our fears. Maybe I could be a brain surgeon. Maybe I could do anything I damn well set my mind to. Nothing is stopping me but my thoughts about it.

I came home that night and told Jeff, "Mr. Marriott thinks I could be a surgeon."

"Do you want to be a surgeon?"

"Nope. But if I wanted to, I could. That's all."

Jeff smiled. "Yes, you could."

When I was in high school, my parents encouraged community college. A four-year university always seemed a bit out of reach. I couldn't see it at the time, but my vision for myself was pretty small. But little by little, I did it. I stumbled through all the classes and requirements for my name to be typed on a ten-inch by twelve-inch paper framed in hideous mahogany. I became the first one in my family to graduate with a Bachelor's degree. Twelve years and hoards of student loans. But it eventually happened. The ceremony was scheduled right after I'd given birth to Evan in 2013. It was 107 degrees. I had nothing to wear and opted for a maternity dress under my graduation gown. I enjoyed the ceremony by spending the entire day with both the gown and maternity dress up around my neck trying to breastfed my fussy baby while my sister held her coat over me to give me privacy and save everyone from seeing my maternity Spanx. It's been six years, and I have no idea where my framed degree is.

But it doesn't matter. The point is that through the trials, I kept showing up for myself, even when I didn't realize it. And, I let others speak into my life. I think God sees how much we struggle with limiting beliefs about what we can accomplish and weaves people into the fabric of our days to drop little hints that stretch our notions of who we are or who we could become into something grander than we could have imagined without them. Like Mr. Marriott.

9. Downsizing Artificial

On New Year's Eve 2010, in my favorite red dress, Jeff and I danced the night away at an art gallery party in D.C. Less than an hour in, I'd coat-checked my stilettos because walking in five-inch heels is not natural and, in fact, quite stupid. So I shimmied around barefoot on the cement floor and let loose to the Black Eyed Peas.

Closing in at midnight, the entire party counted down. Ten...nine...eight. At the stroke of midnight, Jeff drew me in for a kiss. When I shifted my head, my eyes still sparkling, I saw he was holding a red velvet box pulled from his suit pocket.

"Honey, will you marry me?"

I was speechless and pulled his head down for a kiss.

"Does that mean, yes?"

I nodded intensely like a ridiculous bobblehead doll. It was all so perfect, mostly because I'd get to spend my life with a guy I loved and genuinely admired. But also because, in the midst of planning other people's weddings, I could design my own.

If there is such a thing as a 12-step program for the hopelessly, wedding obsessed, I would not only join but likely be president. It's been my thing since I was a little girl. At the age of nine, I begged my dad to let me wash his gold Nissan Sentra. I would carefully vacuum the inside, which always smelled of burnt black coffee and metal shavings from his job. Then I grabbed a bucket and soap and got to work on the outside because afterwards, I knew he would take me to the grocery store and let me pick out a magazine. My choice was predictable, always the newest issue of *Bride's* magazine. I spent the following days pouring over every small detail: the lace dresses and buttercream cakes and music lists. But mostly the flowers.

I'm going to admit, upfront, I don't loathe people who don't buy cut flowers. I loathe the ones who believe flowers are a total waste of money because they die. Well, humans die too, and we still appreciate their existence and beauty, right? I sometimes think, as a society, we don't value beauty like we should because it doesn't last forever. Yes, beauty is fleeting, but maybe if we can permit enjoyment of fleeting beauty with a few cut flowers, we'll teach ourselves to see it in people passing through our lives.

In my early event planning days, I worked with flowers. I've personally designed a few hundred wedding bouquets carried down aisles all over Southern California. I love orchids and roses and even the lowbrow carnations, but without contest, my favorites are the classics: hydrangeas, roses, peonies, and tulips. I swoon every time.

As I pulled the flowers together, shaping them into something beautiful, I noticed that flowers are like women, alluring on their own, but stunning together, each testy in her own way. A hydrangea is endlessly thirsty. She'll soak it all up. And while we love her, she's a tad high maintenance. A rose is classic like Grace Kelly, but before she can be placed, she must be stripped of thorns and left alone for a few days for her petals to open and show her full beauty. A peony is finicky. She's remarkable when she opens up, but she's always a gamble. She might open. She might not. And there's not much you can do about it.

But the most profound one is a tulip. If you make a wedding bouquet with tulips, don't assemble it until the morning of the wedding. Otherwise, you'll craft this perfectly round bouquet, and the tulips, well, they don't realize they need to stay put.

The other flowers are cut and placed in a comfortable spot in the arrangement, and they stop growing. However, the tulip, even after she's been cut, will continue to rise up. Every single flower, stunning, yet the tulip, awkward and unstoppable, keeps growing until she no longer fits in. Her place is on her own.

In 2007, I attended a symposium for weddings, and I was staying at the J.W. Marriott Resort and Spa, in Desert Springs, a far stretch from my typical Holiday Inn budget. Celebrity wedding designers Sylvia Weinstock and Preston Bailey were the headliners.

For all the women over 50 who don't believe they can start over, Sylvia Weinstock is a tulip if I've ever seen one. With her pixie cut white hair, and thick, black-rimmed glasses, she would tell you that if she could start over, anyone, at any age, in any season can start over. When she retired from teaching, she took up a hobby designing cakes. She practiced rolling, and painting sugar pressed flowers until they looked real. She and her husband would have dinner parties, and she'd put a vase out with both real flowers and the sugar flowers she made and then ask the guests if they could point out the fake. She didn't give up until they couldn't tell the difference between her candy flowers and the real ones. Now she is 85 and still making cakes for celebrities. They call her the Leonardo da Vinci of cakes. How's that for a tulip?

After her talk, I headed to a special wedding luncheon, not part of the standard conference. I paid an extra hundred dollars to attend, so I wanted to hurry there and get a good seat. As it started, I walked the room, admiring the arrangements. It was a full house of top designers and wannabes like me.

"Hey, you…" someone whispered.

I looked around but didn't see who.

The voice whispered again, "Hey, you…".

I spotted a crazy woman rigidly moving her hands to signal me like a spy making a covert drop.

Certifiable? Maybe, but I smiled and walked over.

"Sweetie, there's a hole in your skirt."

Wait. What? Oh, dear God.

I ran to the bathroom, where I found my skirt seam ripped open, about seven inches, making today the worst day to wear a floss thong. I had nothing, nada, to cover up my derriere now on display to the entire event planning world. I stretched my shirt as low as possible and tried to find the elevator. I sprinted down hall after hall, cursing the J.W. Marriott for being the size of Monterey. I would have never had this problem at a Holiday Inn. In the midst, my phone rang. It was Stefanie. I shrieked to her in a whisper while I passed a large group of symposium attendees. Then I tripped over the tiniest wrinkle possible in the carpet. My purse crashed to the ground, and all my things rolled on the floor in twelve different directions.

I scrambled to grab everything, maintaining exactly zero dignity and aimed to take shelter in the elevator. I pulsed the elevator button as if it would come faster if I hit it multiple times after it already was summoned. I was telling Stefanie what was happening,

"Everybody… yep, totally humiliated…my entire ass…"

The elevator doors slid open like Broadway curtains, and standing right inside was none other than headliner Preston Bailey.

I whispered into the phone, "I'll call you back." I hung up before she could respond.

At that point, I wanted to BE Preston Bailey. He's a fantastic artist and a loved event planner to the famous, praised for designing and transforming party rooms into little pieces of heaven by using more flowers than the Rose Bowl parade. No joke. Hundreds of thousands of flowers at each event. Floor to ceiling, covered. I'm pretty sure he covers everything but the toilet seats in flowers, but I've never been to the bathroom at his parties, so it's not outside the realm. And now, he was riding the elevator with me. I tried not to be all fan-girly but didn't want to miss this moment talking to him. I stepped in cautiously, backing my ripped skirt up to the elevator wall.

"Where are you headed?" he asked.

"Um, back to my room, to change. I had an accident. Ah, not an accident, accident. I mean, my skirt ripped." My cheeks flushed.

"No, dear. What floor?"

"Oh, yes, seven, please. I love your work."

Preston smiled and tapped the button. I had to make this time count.

"So, where do you find your inspiration?" I finally worked up the nerve to ask.

"All around. Nature. Fashion." He waved his arms around.

"Oh, that's awesome."

Followed by silence, and then it was over.

I wanted to ask how he does it all, a question too big for an elevator ride.

He was so gracious and wished my event business well as he left me with a Hollywood style kiss on the cheek. I fumbled back to my room to change my skirt and called Stefanie back to apologize and tell her about my elevator ride.

I did hear him speak once about the process of covering entire rooms in flowers, a tedious task that takes hundreds of hands, and even more hours. He explained one of his secrets was using fake flowers for the taller areas because they're out of reach and people don't realize they're fake. But where flowers are within reach, if you can physically reach out and touch it, like on dining tables, they must always be real.

"Nobody wants to sit with fakes," he said.

This advice has dimensions that reach beyond flowers. It's a good life lesson to make sure those within our reach and who we spend the most time with are real. You only need to scroll *Facebook* to see there's a whole lot of artificial going around. Every day my newsfeed is full of flawless photos: kids who never meltdown or have diaper explosions and their husbands do all the laundry and shower them with unicorn-kissed roses every day. They post their vacation pictures and shiny, new cars with a giant red bow on the hoods and every annoying time they lose weight. These are the flowers you can see but not touch.

Sometimes I find myself trying to zone out of my life. I will open *Facebook* and scroll and scroll, trying to feel better. It helps precisely zero percent because these posts might not be wholly fake, but they are 100% curated. It would do me right to remember they are the flowers you can see but not touch. The times I ignore this notion, I sink deeper into loneliness or frustration unless I realize what I actually need is human connection. A coffee date. A phone call. A warm embrace. To sit at the table within arm's reach of someone real. Someone willing to be open, to listen and learn, and to share her truth with me.

Despite being outgoing, I'm terrible at small talk. I want to know where you were born, how you were raised, what books you are reading, what are your quirks, what makes you tick and mostly I want to know what you think about God and how you arrived there.

Boundaries are not my strong point. If we're standing in the grocery line, I want you to tell me what you think about life and purpose and how you make sense of all this. I want to hear the best parts and the worst. I hope I've never scared anyone off with my lack of restraint. On a flight from Minnesota to California, I met a woman named Jane, who like me, was okay skipping the small talk. The people around us likely believed we'd known each other for years. We talked about hard relationships and goals and life lessons. That's how I do it.

My best friends all know this about me. While I can talk about the weather, I don't want to. I have a few friends who, despite having spent so much time together, I don't really know them. These women are like summer roses refusing to open or perfectly postured, too tall to reach. I've never had an authentic glimpse of who they are, but I'll keep trying because in sharing my highs and lows, they will eventually open up, or run off scared. It's not wrong to have surface friendships, people in the distance, slightly artificial, but I know now with more clarity than ever, if someone is going to sit at the table with me, it has to be real every time.

10. Downsizing My First Marriage a Second Time

During our engagement, Jeff and I lived together. In sin. There was another couple in our church, newly engaged and living together too.

They tried to say, "Oh, but we don't do, um, ya know. We keep a separation pillow in between us."

I'm pretty sure they were joking, but their Southern accents are downright hard to read. Everything they say sounds obscenely Baptist and godly. Jeff and I had no separation pillow, and we would wake up most mornings tangled up in love.

A relationship after a divorce is hard work. Especially if your first marriage involved abuse or cheating, or both if your ex was an overachiever like mine. Before I met Jeff, in the back of my mind, I worried I would pick the wrong person again. It happens all the time. Women go from one bad relationship to another, hoping for something different. Yet each relationship mirrors the one before because we usually have a type, and the cycle continues.

They say that second marriages are doomed to be harder than the first because you've already decided you're a person who is okay with giving up. I've heard pastors feed this notion by quoting fear-inducing statistics during their sermons. Like people who cohabitate before marriage are more likely to divorce. Or second marriages are 75% likely to end in divorce. Fun stuff. People told me the grass isn't greener on the other side. And my biggest fear was that they would be right because I had given up everything betting on greener pastures.

I had a mental list of what I wanted. From the get-go, trust was non-negotiable. Trust. It seems so cliche. Who doesn't want trust? Should we even have to say it? Isn't it part of the purpose of being in a relationship? To lean on each other and expect certitude. Maybe not. Just in case, I added it to my list. Second, loyalty, which should fall under the same unspoken category as trust. But since I had to add trust, I also added loyalty. I needed true devotion. I couldn't be with someone whose eyes would fix on every skirt passing by, and I would never be okay in a relationship where I felt consumed to check his computer history, text messages or create a fake social media account to spy on him, because who does this? Broken women do.

Since Jeff checked all the boxes, I thought our relationship would be smooth sailing. What I didn't realize was all the wounds from the verbal and emotional abuse of my first marriage had only started to heal. Experts say you should heal past wounds before jumping into a new relationship, but I can tell you for sure it's nearly impossible. You can only go so far on your own. I waited two years after my divorce before I met Jeff. I was as patched up as I could be, but the wounds of hurt and rejection resurfaced when I moved in with Jeff. On one of our early dates, I told Jeff about my divorce and just enough details to not scare him off. I didn't want to drag us down with old baggage. I thought my censorship would keep my past demons away from the new relationship.

Before, I had dealt with name-calling, screaming, and demeaning behavior. I changed my whole way of living to adapt to this kind of love, desperately searching for happiness in a failing marriage and trying not to rock the boat. I think the real damage done in an abusive relationship isn't the actual abuse, but how much you change your life to accommodate it. You tiptoe around everything, at every corner, waiting for the boogie man to jump out and tell you where you're screwing up. Always second-guessing myself left me watching how other people's relationships looked. I would hold up an ungraspable tape measure to see how I added up and where I needed improvement. Not once did the measuring tape tell me I was ahead of the game. Never. Second-guessing turns into third-guessing and endlessly looking to fix me.

In my new relationship, the questions about my self-worth would arise, and I would take them to the plate one at a time. In the beginning, this wasn't easy. I doubted myself at every turn. I feared I was too needy, or I would say the wrong things. That I wasn't interesting enough. Or when we went out, I worried I would end up embarrassing him with the clothes I wore, or my body shape, or my words. I was always waiting for the other shoe to drop and had constant anxiety leftover from an abusive relationship.

In the beginning, I made sure I always had enough cash in the bank to leave should there be any sign of offense from Jeff. Name-calling, yelling, I waited for it, but it never came. Because Jeff is kind and good, and at his very core, he has the best intentions for us. Still, my PTSD would leave me over apologizing to him for not having things cleaned up and in order before he got home. Not that Jeff ever asked me to do any of these things, but because it was so ingrained in me from my first marriage and all the church reminders of a woman's place in the house. But Jeff couldn't care less. Which I should have known because the first time I went to his apartment when we were dating, there were piles of sports gear and mountains of clothes everywhere and a stack of dishes so high it rivaled Mount Kilimanjaro.

"Did the rapture happen?" I teased him.

Still, I stressed about all these things.

I had this moment one night, after Jeff and I got into an argument. In tears and very pregnant, I drove to the grocery store to pick up some standard loathing food, ice cream, or chocolate, or a pound of sugar, maybe all of it. I needed to talk to someone. My first instinct was to hold everything in, to keep quiet. I had been trained to keep all arguments a secret to protect the marriage, but now, in the store parking lot, I called my mom and vented on how frustrated I was. At first, I didn't want to tell her. It felt like I was betraying Jeff when she asked me.

"What happened, honey?"

I hesitated but then said, "I shouldn't say this, but, uh, we got into a fight over our clothes. Well, my clothes."

"Your clothes?"

"I've told Jeff not to put wet towels in the laundry basket. And he still does it, even though I've told him, like a million times, how it makes all my clothes damp and gross and I hate it."

My first feelings were embarrassment and shame at my lack of ability to handle something so tedious in marriage. My second feeling was fear that Jeff would find out I told my mom about the towel argument and get angry. But I reminded myself this wasn't my first marriage. Just when I had finished venting, an enormous feeling of relief and freedom washed over me. And then I realized what I was upset about.

"Towels?" my mom asked softly.

I paused, feeling suddenly lighter. "Towels."

We both laughed.

It wasn't lost on me, or her, that I was upset over wet towels. Yes, gross and wet towels but towels, just the same. Not being yelled at or belittled or called five-letter names. Not given the cold shoulder or having a hole punched in the wall. Not being controlled or criticized. Not dealing with the discovery of yet another woman. Wet towels. I realized how wonderfully boring and romantic this fight was over these gross wet towels. The next day I went shopping and bought a deluxe laundry bin on wheels with three compartments: his, hers, and towels. Who needs counseling when you have organizational bins? At Christmas, I unwrapped my mom's gift for me. An Egyptian cotton towel set in royal blue.

Second marriages are a lot of work but not as hard as living with an abuser. Mainly, second marriages are hard because you have to unlearn all the adaptations you had formed in the first marriage when you were trying to stay in a relationship that constantly demeaned who you are as a person, a woman, and an equal partner. Abuse can make it hard to relearn what it is like to be loved and known.

> Tim Keller says, "To be loved but not known is comforting but superficial. To be known and not loved is our greatest fear. But to be fully known and truly loved is, well, a lot like being loved by God. It is what we need more than anything. It liberates us from pretense, humbles us out of our self-righteousness, and fortifies us for any difficulty life can throw us."

People talk about coming into a marriage with unrealistic expectations, but this time, I had come under-expecting. I hoped we would fall into a pace where we complemented each other, but I under-expected the precious, honest friendship that would grow. I under-expected his sincere commitment to love me, not as an obligation, but because he treasures me. Jeff was so patient and gentle with my heart. There were times I wasn't able to explain things to him because I was still figuring them out myself, and he offered me compassion at every turn. Layer by layer, I've had to peel back the things I learned in the first go-round and relearn what marriage should be. Every morning, I still wake up tangled in Jeff's arms. I'm deeply thankful to walk this path of life with him. In the mess, in our shiny wryness, and the moments of romance and passion. I didn't know it could be, and still is so good. I'm grateful for second chances, second marriages, and greener pastures.

11. Reteach the Loveliness

In D.C., I carefully moved my issues with the church to the back burner, and I began to embrace church like I hadn't in a while. The truth was, I had invested my whole life being a churchgoer, and I missed it. I missed communion and worship, and I wanted everything to go back to normal. Looking for a church to join, we visited a modest congregation at a coffee shop, and the service was excellent, but the drive was too long. Looking for something a bit closer, we ventured to the next church. They held Sunday service at a movie theater, less the popcorn and Vin Diesel. It was the growing trend for younger churches to conserve money generally spent on church buildings, which I appreciate, but it felt irreverent singing Hillsong's Oceans after spending last night in the very same seats watching Liam Neeson and Jessica Biel fighting off assassins in the A-Team remake. Finally, we landed at a church in Alexandria, not a far ride from our studio apartment by the Eisenhower metro stop. It was a newer church and pretty impressive. Maybe 700 members. There were dozens of programs, and small groups, and women's ministry, and they generously gave to the community. It seemed nothing was left untouched.

We wanted to connect and help, so I volunteered in the children's church, precisely one time. I discovered I'd sooner get a root canal from a podiatrist than watch other people's kids. Not my strong point. So, I became a church greeter, welcoming people with pens and bulletins, and a friendly smile. Jeff joined the usher team and assisted in collecting the offering. We got involved where we could and spent three months with a study group doing Dave Ramsey's Financial Peace University. This prompted us to use words like *snowball* and *gazelle* regularly, lingo any dedicated Christian should know. We would repeat Dave's famous phrase to each other, something like, "We live like nobody else today so that we can live like nobody else tomorrow."

To meet other couples, we joined a marriage small group held at the studio apartment of a sweet young couple. When we introduced ourselves, my past came back to haunt me when the wife of the young couple introduced herself with the same name and from the same small town as the hussy my ex-husband had cheated with. I had never met the hussy, so this could be her. Talk about choking on my communion wafer. I pasted a smile on my face and said hello. It couldn't possibly be *her,* I told myself. The hussy my ex knew had three kids and was married to a police officer, not a youth pastor. This young woman in front of me had the body of a gymnast, not a mom of three. No, it couldn't have been her.

But to make sure, I asked. "Do you have any kids?"

Nope. No kids. Not the hussy. Onward with the group.

The group was exploring the leading Christian book *Love and Respect* by Dr. Emerson Eggerichs. We were to read the chapters before gathering to discuss them. But when I sat down with the book, my eyes glossed over the words. It was too much structure of what the his-and-her marriage roles should be. It seemed a little critical of women, but the book was so vetted and popular in the church, I must be wrong about it. Still, I couldn't relate to much of what the book was saying. I decided I must have been too preoccupied with my new love, career, and the big city.

For all of our involvement in this new church, my body would tense when the topic of marriage came up. I put up a stone wall fending off any Biblical marriage guidance. One service, I ducked out to the ladies' room when they read Ephesians 5:22, "Wives, submit yourselves to your own husbands." They were reading it all wrong, out of context. Disconnected became my routine for most church services, and it often felt like a courtroom trial. I became an observer. I was actively listening not in accord, more as a witness, sometimes a defendant. These thoughts felt like a betrayal of the church. I grew up believing if the pastor preaches it on Sunday, it must be an inspired word from God. Therefore, it must be right for everyone. Not anymore. During the sermon, I took notes like a Harvard Law student. I was carefully writing down things to look up. Later, I sifted through every word attempting to find any cracks in the theology or signs of risk.

One night, our church small group discussion turned to the subject of homosexuality. A woman shared that her gay colleague had asked her if, as a Christian, she thought being gay was a sin. She was uncertain of how to respond. She didn't want to upset him and asked the group for advice.

Someone spoke up. "I've had this happen. My friend asked me the same thing. My reply was to tell him, the Bible says to love the sinner, hate the sin. I love you but a sin-is-a-sin-is-a-sin." He shrugged his shoulders like he was utterly helpless to the issue and said, "The Bible is very clear. I had to tell him the truth in love." And then added his friend discontinued talking to him after that, shocker.

It was apparent he believed he was doing the proper thing by holding up his Christian beliefs and sharing what he deciphered as the truth of God. And losing a friend who is offended by God's word, well, that was the price we pay to call ourselves Christian. His justification was, yes, people would be offended, but it was still our obligation and burden to share it. It was on point with the evangelical churches I was raised attending. Social martyrdom in the name of Jesus is held in high esteem. If you're not being persecuted, you're not working hard enough.

At that moment, I became keenly aware I'd heard the term, love the sinner, hate the sin, dozens of times, a few specifically aimed at me after my divorce. But now it felt the glass had been shattered. Growing up, I had never accepted the orthodox view that homosexuality is a sin. But never more than in this very moment had I felt such guilt at my impropriety at only truly sensing the damage to others, and primarily the LGBTQ community, after having been on the receiving end of the "love the sinner, hate the sin" creed.

My animosity only simmered, but I sat silently in the group, knowing I was in the minority. I was exasperated. The whole thing troubled me, but right then, I was working to mend my already broken heart and start my life over. I reasoned with myself. I wanted to be in the church and have a clean start with God. At this moment, I didn't have the brain space for it. I was too fragile. I'm ashamed to admit I chose to ignore the doubt waxing so that I could save myself.

The truth was I was terrified of what I might discover if I began looking closer. Cracking open this door, meant a whole slew of other questions would likely come knocking like a Girl Scout during cookie season. If the Bible actually said all of these things and meant them literally, would I be able to stay in the Christian faith? I didn't think so, and I couldn't go there. I shelved my Bible and put on a smiling face. It took me years before I'd pick it up again.

I sat voiceless and doubting. Many of my Christian friends emphatically offered "God's opinion" against homosexually. It appeared to be one of the most pronounced sins. I wonder, why is homosexuality *the* issue? In 2014, World Vision announced they would hire gays and lesbians, and the Christian community flipped out. People lost it. Many called to cancel their support, pulling funds from the starving, undernourished, and dying children. It was a modest price to pay for keeping a moral high ground and making it crystal clear that our Christian values matter more than actual, real-life children with hungry bellies and empty plates. Thoroughly alarmed at the response and to save funding, World Vision recanted two days later.

One night in the fall of 2016, while the rest of the world slept, Lifeway Christian bookstores yanked Jen Hatmaker's books off their shelves when she declared her support and affirmation for the LGBTQ community. The chain bookstore made similar threats to Eugene Peterson after he vaguely mentioned his support of the LGBTQ community but then clarified he didn't. Eugene Peterson, a man who has written over thirty books and one of the most loved versions of the Bible. Years of dedication to God and people and all of his writing would be tossed aside in an instant.

> John Pavlovitz said it well, "That someone like Jen Hatmaker (or Rob Bell before her) could go from poster child to pariah with a few heartfelt sentences is absurd and embarrassing, and for so many people it's more confirmation that Christianity is not worth their time because of the venom it produces. It is for so many people who once called the Church home, but longer do, assurance that they made the right choice."

Lifeway does sell books on gay conversion, including one called *The Homosexual Agenda*, with a description that reads: "'The homosexual agenda's' primary aim is to trump the rights of all other groups, especially those of faith." Their primary agenda? I'm pretty sure they want to have the same rights as the rest of us and perhaps be able to, gasp, order a wedding cake without being thumped over the head with the Bible. While Lifeway does sell many books written by great authors, I find the stance they have repeatedly taken on LGBTQ topics troubling.

Right after a hurricane tore through Houston and right after a group of torch-carrying white Nazis marched in Charlottesville, and right after President Trump said Nazis were good people, a group of evangelical leaders released a public manifesto, called the Nashville Statement, asserting the belief that marriage should only be between a man and a woman. In Article 10 of the declaration, it stated, approving of homosexuality "constitutes an essential departure from Christian faithfulness and witness." and that approval "is a matter of moral indifference." At the heart of this was the idea that if you aren't actively in defense of traditional marriage, you are sinning by your moral indifference.

Yeah, I get it. It wasn't anything new, but the offensiveness of their timing was appalling. Even more so was the part where they collected donations to promote this idea of marriage. Instead of pointing people towards the sick and oppressed, the hurting and dying, they held their mostly white, callously-free hands out to take up an offering. At a time when people were lost, hurt, and homes were flooded, at a time the city was dark without power, Christian leaders like Matt Chandler and Francis Chan, felt the need to take ink to paper to "shine a light into darkness," when what people needed was actual light and electricity. What happened to bear one another's burdens? And the more critical questions, I was asking myself, does Christianity produce more pain than healing?

I think along the way we've gotten lost, made a few wrong turns. Somewhere along the route of hosting recovery groups and church potlucks and Vacation Bible School, we took a shortcut through the land of judgment and absolutes. Somewhere we started to coward behind the illusion of fear, and we have forgotten the loveliness of Jesus. The innermost part of our hearts that see the pure beauty in others. Even those we disagree with.

92

Pulitzer Prize winning-poet, Galway Kinnell wrote: "Sometimes it is necessary to reteach a thing its loveliness."[2]

Has our church slowly traded loveliness to take moral positions in the most unloving ways and to the demise of our highest calling, to love? We can't give something we don't hold freely. We can't share light when our hearts are overshadowed by fear. We can't keep love and understanding when we roll the nuances of theology into our identity. We are a collective. To love and understand others, we must love and understand ourselves. And in the process not shame those learning about who they are and trying to figure out how they fit in. There's no one exact way to be a person.

Why is the church taking a stand where the stance is unnecessary or sinking their heels into an issue without honestly questioning, that perhaps they could be dead wrong? Stand up for something else. Anything else. Please.

Curing cancer.
Heart disease.
The environment.
Forgiveness.
Girls education in underdeveloped countries.
World hunger and malnutrition.
Abused women.
Abused children.
Abused animals.
Human trafficking.
The homeless.
Veterans with PTSD.
The refugee crisis.
Drinking water for all.
Drug addiction crisis.

The foster care system.
Criminal justice reform.
Suicide.
Mental health.
AIDS.
Factory farming.
Illiteracy.
Special needs families.
Energy crisis.

If the church can read this list, which is missing hundreds of issues and hurting people, yet still care more about homosexuality, or worse, using church money to fund a marriage stance while people are hungry and hurting, we have big problems. I can no longer be a silent part of it. We should look at this list and let these issues shake us to our core. Issues where division doesn't live and love would ignite hope. We should stand for these things. How do we brush the dirt aside to uncover the loveliness? How do we spark the deepest level of understanding for all? How do we learn to love fearlessly, like Jesus?

12. Downsizing Sleep

I set all my doubting aside, yet again, because I was now growing a tiny person. To be clear, there was a human being in my belly, and I wanted him out. Precisely nine months and a week past my due date, I was cranky and sore and phoned my midwife. I just knew the baby was never coming out. He would graduate high school still in my womb. I was doing everything to help him along. Primrose oil, bouncing on a yoga ball, eating all the spicy food, having the most uncomfortable sex, and still no baby.

I cried to my midwife, "Maybe I should drink the Castor oil?"

The midwife said it would only give me diarrhea, and the baby would come when he was good and ready. I reluctantly settled against the castor oil and instead took a long walk. That night my water broke, and 32 hours later, I gave birth to Evan.

For all of my insecurities, motherhood was not on the list. I was so confident going into motherhood. So sure it would come naturally. I was raised around dozens of babies, and I knew everything about them. My mom ran a daycare most of my childhood, and my siblings had so many youngsters people would ask us, *Are you Mormon?* No. *Catholic?* No. *Hispanic?* Yep. But all the babysitting in the world could not have equipped me for the monumental assignment of motherhood.

During the first night in the hospital, Evan wouldn't stop crying. I tried nursing and rocking and diaper changing. He just cried and cried. It was nothing like the Huggies commercials. We just knew something was wrong. We called the nurse for help. She held him up, like when Rafiki held up Simba in the Lion King. She looked him over and put him back in my arms, saying he was fine.

In a syrupy drawl, she laughed, "He's just a baby."

Wait. What? Jeff and I looked at each other. We were terrified.

In between diapers and nursing, I was burning the candle at both ends, still working from home and going to school full-time. I hadn't slept in weeks and my post-delivery body, well, it was different. I didn't fit into any clothes. But Evan was precious and perfect, and I was head over heels in love. Despite his sweetness, he was especially fidgety and non-stop fussy. I felt trapped in the apartment, but the second I tried to drive somewhere, he would scream in his car seat. We took him to church with us, and I saw other moms holding their new babies during service too, quietly kissing and snuggling them. But Evan was too fussy for me to sit, and we mostly stopped going to church during this transition, but I didn't mind. I sat at home in my gliding chair with Evan nestled in my arms, and I marveled at the instant, unquestionable love that arrives with a baby.

When Evan was six months old, the Coast Guard gave us the next assignment a few thousand miles away in Washington state. We spent a month driving across the country taking our time and stopping to see the Biltmore in Asheville, and on to Nashville, New Orleans, and a dozen other sites, before we moved to Poulsbo, a quaint Viking sea town, about thirty minutes west of Seattle with charming shops and homes. It could have doubled as a movie set for Pleasantville. Our perfect townhouse was a short walk from Main Street with many downtown eateries and Mom 'n Pop antique shops and where city workers sprinkled water on purple flower beds dangling from steel blue light posts.

Although we instantly felt at home in our new small town, it took some adjusting coming from city life. I was doing my best not to rival my last home town with my new home town, but it can be sticky when making a move. When I moved to D.C., I missed sunny San Diego beaches, the hang-loose community, and real Mexican fare. Now I missed D.C.'s grandeur, endless career opportunities, and, even though I was grappling spiritually, I missed our church. I told myself to stay present because both skipping ahead and looking back is wasteful. An indulgence we can't afford in life. I did my best to live this out and focus on my precious baby boy. I grasped to early morning feedings and Evan's first steps. I would brush my lips on his soft head and inhale his sweet baby fragrance and meditate to his soft snoring.

Right before I left Washington D.C., my friendships were just starting to move to the level beyond the facade of fake niceties, and I was making great connections. I resolved it wouldn't take me so long in Poulsbo. I had one class left to finish my degree, and I still was doing freelance marketing. Keep It Together and Don't Drop The Ball were my daily affirmations. But my anxiety was skyrocketing, and Evan was waking a dozen times a night.

At home, without family or friends nearby, I channeled everything I had left into trying to keep up the house. While Jeff was busy acclimating to his new assignment, I was determined to find my new community. One Sunday, a gal from church stopped me on my way out and invited me to a mom's group. The women were sweet and welcoming, but I was still a foreigner in a small town. I learned a lesson all must come to learn when moving to a small town. Everybody is genuinely sweet as pie, but none of them will want to be your friend. I realized in a big city, like D.C., hundreds of people move in and out, all day long. There's never a shortage of people ready to make friends. But in a small town, where families have deep roots and already-in-place friendships, some going back several generations, being a newcomer is tough. Many of the women were already content with their friendship routines. Although they set a high bar for being friendly, they didn't need connection beyond social niceties.

Loneliness filled the cracks in the first few months, notably when I would hear of a play date or mom's night out I wasn't invited to. I knew this wasn't me. Usually, I'm okay on my own, and I only felt sadder at my desperation and pettiness. But since I had come intending to make fast friends, and since I was drowning with the new challenges of momming, I felt empty. It was a flashback to junior high and the frivolous carnation-gram fundraiser. Your friends paid a buck, and a volunteer would stand at the front of the homeroom and announce if someone sent you a single-stemmed carnation, a marker of friendship, popularity, and mean girls. But still, I wanted one.

There was one mom who I admired from afar. I saw her *Facebook* posts with the right blend of humor, wisdom, and self-depreciation. I needed to be her friend. She was also a photographer, and I booked her for a mini-family session. We didn't have any professional photos of us from the time Evan was born, and he was almost one year old. Also, I sensed the likelihood I wouldn't be able to recall this blurry part of life, and I wanted it documented with a few photos. The kind of pictures that in three decades I will look back on with nostalgic affection and remember only the gooey baby kisses and wonderfulness of a new family bonding. Three decades in which my mind would forget the endless puke, poop, and sleepless nights. Those kinds of photos.

Getting ready for the day was laborious because Evan had started walking and roaming into everything I hadn't yet childproofed. Jeff was irritable because he hates having his photo taken, and I was drained. I scoured my closet trying to find something my body would jostle into, leaving a mountain of too-small clothes on my bed, one more thing to clean up later. And I was on the verge of a breakdown. I wasn't sure why, but maybe because I hadn't slept in a year. I settled on a long gold sweater atop a too-worn black dress and elected to tease my hair. The bigger my hair, the less likely people would see my body. Plus, a little volume never hurt anyone.

Driving to our neighborhood park for the photoshoot, I struggled to keep the baby awake, trying my best by shaking his foot and talking loudly to him. Simultaneously as we pulled into the parking spot, Evan's sleepy eyes glued shut, and grey clouds in the sky opened up and started spitting. A few minutes out of the car, my big hair writhed into the shape of a Bob Ross Chia Pet. We went ahead with the photos because it was a miracle we had made it there, but when I got the pictures back, I was immediately disappointed. I could see the tiredness in my face, and our super serious baby had refused to smile in every photo. I felt the entire weight of the photoshoot, and my too large body, and every single flaw seemed to intensify.

I sent my photographer friend an email, like, *Hey, I'm not really happy with the photos.* We went back and forth a little. I was grumpy and regrettably killed any chance of becoming friends with her. Truth be told, it wasn't the photos I was disappointed with, but deep down, I was disheartened with myself. I was angry because I didn't recognize myself in the images. Not just physically but mentally and spiritually. I had no idea how I fit into this new town. And motherhood. And life. I just felt lost.

13. Downsizing a Drifting Identity

Many working moms would give their right arm to stay home with their babies, but I missed working. Not working from home, but putting on a dress and heels and going somewhere. A place, where for a few hours, I didn't have to put my nose up to the butt of a baby's diaper and sniff to see if it was time for a changing. I traded business lunches and happy-hour cocktails for mid-night nursing sessions and savory slow-cooker recipes. And while I loved my baby more than anything, it wasn't about him. It was about me. I struggled with finding value and worth outside a career, even while working from home, and I was searching frantically to find my way, yet again, in a new town. I'd meet moms who seemed happy being home, leaving me questioning even more why I felt lost. But once in a while, I'd meet a dear, stay-at-home-mama, who seemed a little lost like me. Without me asking, she would confess her career path or education and sheepishly, make an excuse why she was not working and using her skills. Together we would grasp tiny threads of the women we once were as our hearts would shake with the suspicion we weren't doing something significant enough, or truly using our education, or that we were becoming irrelevant.

Without a job, was I just a mom? A wife? Was this my mid-life crisis? If it was, it showed up like Christmas ornaments in September. It was time to figure this all out. I had overheard a hippy lady at the grocery store talking about meditation and inner peace and finding your chi. It seemed nice. Maybe that's what I needed. So after I delicately laid Evan for his nap, I perched down on my bedroom floor and attempted to be silent. But my laundry was giving me dirty looks, and I needed to catch up on Married at First Sight, and it's undesirable to meditate while sitting on stodgy, beige carpet. I needed peregrine hardwood floors with vases of purple orchids and candles and Reiki Zen meditation music as I honed my inner spirit. But alternatively, my mind would roam to the ugly tan carpet, and my German Shepherd would relentlessly march up to lick my face.

The trepidation I felt while trying to be alone with my thoughts was like being forced to have dinner with a group of extended family who all spoke a different language. It's awkward, and everyone is hesitant because we don't understand each other. My hands are clammy and unsure, pushing a fork across my plate, trying to make small talk with all the different parts of myself I could not communicate with.

"How long have you lived here?" I'd ask.

And they'd look at each other smiling and then back to me, nodding in a sure reply, "Yes."

I looked at the clock and sighed.

But I wanted something to tell me who I was. On came the tests to see if I was sanguine or melancholic or phlegmatic (which always makes me think of excess mucus). Perhaps knowing that I'm an ENFJ, or Enneagram 4 wing 3, or an introvert with ambivert tendencies would help me show up better.

Joining a local mom's group, I would meet potential new friends and found they would introduce themselves with their name and one of three things: their roles, their heritage, or their religion. But mostly by their roles. Wife, mom, nurse, teacher, lawyer.

But there was something that caused me to pause about using roles to define my identity. Maybe because it seemed so fleeting and after having the rug pulled from under my career path as quickly as it started, it just didn't seem safe anymore. And because life changes faster than I can jump off the scale at my doctor's office. One day you're wearing Michael Kors dresses and helping plan the Presidential Inauguration luncheon, and the next, you're wearing week-old yoga pants and reading *Llama Llama Red Pajama* for the one-millionth time.

My identity? It could be I'm a mutt- a compilation of my baby-obsessed mother, who asks once a week when I'm going to have another baby; the hair-raising Pentecostal church we attended when I was young, where people speaking in tongues would pass out on the floor while another member covers them with a blanket; and my bachelors degree, that took me twelve years to finish. I could be bits and pieces of my achievements, failures, thoughts, and memories. Or maybe I'm just the last picture I posted on Facebook that's racked up 23 likes.

I spent just over a decade in the event planning industry and missed it terribly. One Monday morning in 2007, after a weekend wedding expo for my business, I got a call. At the time, I was fending off beginning signs of the recession and continually fighting with my now ex-husband because I suspected he was talking to his old girlfriend. And I was about 40 pounds overweight. I was in the middle of emailing a reply to one of my brides who wanted to change the color of ribbon, yet again, this time from neutral champagne to dusty oatmeal, when my business line rang. It was a gal inquiring about her wedding. I was on the west coast, and her sweet southern voice stood out like tangy barbecue sauce on sushi. She told me she was getting married and we had met the day before at the wedding expo. I couldn't remember her because there were close to 900 brides. She wanted to hire me for her wedding.

"I just had a good feeling about working with you, because you're like me, a bigger girl."

I choked. I must have heard wrong. Did she call me a *bigger girl?* My voice paralyzed. I'm pretty sure this falls under the category of things you can say about yourself but not others. I didn't end up working with this bride, but I did spend the next year thinking maybe if I wasn't a *bigger girl* my marriage would get better.

After divorcing, I kept my ex's last name for a short while because I was professionally tied to it and didn't want to tell the brides I was working with my name changed because my marriage failed. My last name wasn't horrible, but it started with the letter S, which made my initials A.S.S. Really if that wasn't a sign of what was to come, I don't know. When I remarried, I was hesitant about taking on someone else's name again. I thought about going back to my maiden name, but it didn't feel quite right. I thought about picking a brand new last name like Cheryl Strayed. I could be Angela Adventure or have a first name, like Cher. Ultimately I decided to take Jeff's last name and start anew. A new marriage, a new city, and a new name. I felt it was symbolic because I had changed so much, and just as I've grown as a person, I'd be able to grow into this new name.

If anything can send you into a tailspin trying to find your identity, it's motherhood. Every one of my friends tells me they feel like they've lost something in motherhood. Well, the honest ones do. Where did that girl go? It's something I can't quite put my finger on, but I have a heavy feeling she's not coming back. Marianne Williamson said, "When a woman gives birth, two are born; a baby is born from the womb of its mother, and a woman is born from the womb of her former existence."

Maybe Stella never got her groove back. Perhaps she just found a different dance. For far too long, I've walked around lamenting and looking for the part of me that is lost. But maybe she is not so much lost as departed. Like an overdramatic goodbye love scene, I see her telling me, "My time has come to leave. You are strong enough and don't need me anymore. You need to move on, press forward, and love the woman you've become." To grieve who I was before is healthy and natural, but a dangerous trap is living with the denial that she's coming back. Perhaps it's time to let her go, live in the present and learn to fall in love with the woman I am now.

If my early mid-life crisis has taught me anything, it's that we cannot be guilted or shamed into an identity. Guilt and shame build our ego, not our identity. Our ego is the labels we assign ourselves. We enforce these labels with our thoughts. Our thoughts impress on everything. And the most fantastic thing is that we command our thoughts. I heard someone say, you are not who you think you are. And it's so accurate.

Downsizing our identity means realizing that identity is not made of our thoughts. Our identity isn't what our family and friends think we are. It's not our hourglass or pear body shape or being a *bigger girl*. It's not measured by society, our achievements, jobs, performances, education level, city, family, relationships, friends, community, our social media profiles, or the things we own. It's not our past choices but the lessons we take from them. It's not just our stories but the way we choose to tell them. It's a collection of the unique values we bring, our character, our contradictions. Identity isn't essential because it's how others see us, but it's vital because it's how we see ourselves, and thus it's the lens with which we see the whole world.

14. Downsizing Love and Respect

As we settled into our two-story sage green townhouse in perfect Washington state, we began scouting for a church. Some name the act of bouncing around from church to church, trying to find one that fits, church-shopping. I prefer to call it church-dating. I wasn't expecting a church soulmate, but I wanted a church with chemistry but also one who wouldn't try to feel me up on the first date. Equally as important, it would be welcoming and not play hard-to-get because who has time for that? Not me.

Our first Sunday morning at a new church, everything was off to a good start. The worship was typical. Someone made announcements, and then two pastors started talking from the pulpit. At first, I assumed it was more announcements. But they just kept going right into the teaching. How strange was this? The entire service they preached in tandem. It was a little awkward to watch because the styles didn't mesh. In the church-dating relationship, it was like the guy who insists on bringing his mom on the honeymoon. It's just too many people.

We kept dating around and descended on a small church held at another movie theater. The church was a newer start-up. There were no fancy lights or perfectly orchestrated worship bands like in D.C., but the service was friendly and unpolished. After a few Sundays, we were ready to take it to the next dating level and joined a small group. This is where real church happens, sitting around someone's kitchen table with chips and guacamole and an odd collection of people from the congregation. Single. Married. All ages. Mixed races. Kids. No kids. Coming together to build relationships and try to understand how to live better.

This particular group was for couples with kids, but it met at six in the evening, right about Evan's bedtime. We usually hired a sitter. In our first meeting, the group leader announced we would be reading the book *Love and Respect* by Dr. Emerson Eggerichs, the same book from the D.C. small group that I didn't connect with and thought it was even a bit suppressive. I was probably wrong. There are many things I'm usually wrong about, like first impressions, gym fashion, and picking a sweet cantaloupe from the produce section. I can never remember, should the melon have a yellow spot, or was it a green spot? I always have to ask the produce person who is never any help.

Once a woman saw the produce worker brush me off. She strolled up to me, "Baby girl, you gotta sniff it." She held it up to her face. "If it smells sweet, it usually is."

I thanked her as I drew the cantaloupe to my face. I now sniff each cantaloupe before I commit. I'm getting better but now and then I still pick a bad one. So it shouldn't surprise anyone, least myself, that I could be wrong about this *Love and Respect* book. Actually, I wanted to be incorrect. I wanted to get back to fitting in and having a manual for something clear to strive for, like the perfect marriage.

Plus, I was in a better place now. New state. New church. New season. I had a husband who dearly loved me, and I loved him. We were doing our best to pray, both together and for each other, and walk through muddy waters of life and church and wet towel arguments. I thought, just maybe, I was healed enough I could return to the church. I was excited to learn new tools and anchor our marriage to God's plan.

The first meeting was only introductions and getting the reading schedule, approximately two to three chapters a week. The day before we gathered again, I laid Evan down for a nap, clasped a giant cup of hot coffee, and opened the book. The theory was laid out in the beginning; Women have one primary need - to be loved. And men have one primary need - to be respected. The author said he felt there are a ton of books telling men to be more loving but not enough telling women to be respectful towards their husbands, and he believed this lack of resources was a grave disservice. Something inside of me was waving a red flag. I didn't know if it was the negative tone towards women or his idea that if women stopped nagging, men would behave more lovingly.

I urged myself to press on. Give it a fair shot. Don't let my past close me off to God's message for marriage. But the little hairs on my neck stood up when I scanned:

> "I want to remind all husbands that their wives are basically good-willed women. They are only acting critical, contentious, and disrespectful because they are crying out for love." (Page 81).

Seriously? Are strong-willed women acting out disrespectfully because we are begging for love, or do we want mutual respect? I was back in the ugly green chair, in my first marriage, sitting across from the pastor telling me to be more submissive. I was completely ruffled. The next day at the group, I debated staying quiet because we were new to the church and trying to make friends. And all the churches talk about good wives having a gentle and quiet spirit. But despite the book's advice to remain silent and submissive, it is not my nature. I cautiously admitted I was struggling to accept the concepts as they were written. Sexist is what they were. My friend Ashleyann, one of the strongest, calls-it-like-she-sees-it people, spoke up.

"Well, I must be a man because respect is most important to me too."

Another person also admitted they thought it was gender bias. A few people in the group believed we were misinterpreting the message of the book. According to them, we were missing the part where it was meant to protect our marriage. I half expected this response. Most of the book's guidance was typical to traditional marriage teaching in the church, and several people dismissed the ones of us who spoke out.

We continued gathering over potluck dinners, with simple foods like spaghetti and tacos to feed our small crowd. It was time for Lent, and even though I'm not Catholic and have never celebrated Lent before, I decided to give up meat and animal products for the full 40 days. I would not advise anyone to go vegan during a spiritual impasse. I'm not going to lie; being vegan was great until it was not, which happened around day two. Butter topped the list of things I missed the most, especially when you add sugar and slather it on a warm cupcake. Towards the end of Lent, I was desperate. Ashleyann knew this and had brought a pack of store-bought cupcakes, but only after taking a black sharpie to all the ingredients and then promising me, they were for sure vegan, because that's what friends do. We continued reading the book and meeting to discuss it.

I flinched when I read Eggerich's ideas on women's position in the home and motherhood:

> "Adam doesn't expect Eve to have a baby and hand the baby back to him so she can go back to work. Those who advocate domestic equality promote this idea." (Page 200).

Huh? Did the publishers mistakenly drop a script from Mad Men in this book? We should let the men smoke cigars in the parlor, while the women take lessons from a submissive Stepford wife. If a woman disagrees on an issue with her husband, the author quotes the classic verse, 1 Timothy 2:12: Women are not allowed to exercise authority over a man but are to remain quiet. The book pushes further that women should be quiet in a dignified way, not pouty or sour. Keep quiet and look pretty while doing it. But the part that made my blood turn hot was when he shares a letter he received from a woman who had been physically and verbally abused by her husband,

> "... [she] had gone back to him after he repented, realized she hadn't completely forgiven him and certainly wasn't showing him respect. After coming across our materials, she began showing him respect, — mostly by remaining quiet and dignified instead of arguing. Their relationship improved considerably..." (Page 278).

If one person has to suffocate and bend and keep her mouth shut for the marriage to work, it's not a marriage. It's a hierarchy. Of course, we have the choice to remain quiet, but to make silence akin to having a happy marriage is flat wrong. It's stifling and suppressive towards women and #timesup.

Hundreds of churches have promoted this book, seemingly without caution and with the absence of much-needed caveats. This book is popular because it has woven truths into falseness and misrepresents what marriage should look like. It's American Christianity at its lowest. For me, it was the marriage edition of *How to Kiss Dating Goodbye*. Maybe I should have taken warning when I saw that Focus on the Family was a sponsor of the book. In his book, *Love Must Be Tough* 2010 edition, Focus on the Family founder

James Dobson answers a letter from a woman named Laura who's married to a man with a violent temper. He's a church leader and well respected, and he also beats her with his fists. Her concern is that the beatings are becoming more frequent and more violent, and it's all her fault because she's provoking him. She's tired of staying home to hide her bruises.

He says she can get a divorce, but he doesn't believe this is the solution. "Our purpose should be to change her husband's behavior, not kill the marriage" (page 160). He suggests his love-must-be-tough response and breaking out of this cycle while "she's still young enough to cope with the consequences." Meaning, young enough to take a few beatings? He suggests forcing a crisis, refusing his consent, and "let him rage if he must" (page 161). In the hope that baiting him into a violent situation will allow a path to Christian counseling and reconciliation.

In the next few paragraphs, he says he's seen many cases where the women bait the husband into hitting them:

> "Because females are just as capable of hatred and anger as males, and a woman can devastate a man by enticing him to strike her. It is a potent weapon. Once he has lost control and lashed out at his tormentor, she then sports undeniable evidence of his cruelty. She can show her wounds to her friends who gasp at the viciousness of that man. She can press charges against him in some cases and have him thrown in jail. She can embarrass him at his work or in the church. In short, by taking a beating, she instantly achieves a moral advantage in the eyes of neighbors, friends, and the law." (Page 163)

Taking a beating gives us a moral advantage? I don't remember Jesus saying this. For sure, it was left out of my Sunday School felt-board lessons.

Another prominent Christian author, Joyce Meyer, has an article on her website, called the *Truth of Prayer*, where she tells a story of a great pastor, who before he became a pastor, was terrible to his wife. He'd lock her out of the house, and she'd have to sleep on the porch. And when he decided to let her in, since she was a Godly woman, she'd smile cheerily and make him breakfast. Meyer writes,

> "She was a godly example for him. She prayed for him and God gave her the grace to be good to him in spite of his rude behavior. And because she continued to be so good to him, he eventually came to know the Lord and was radically changed. As a result, he became one of the greatest preachers who ever lived. That's the power of prayer."

Misogyny and abuse is the base of the power of prayer? This was the tip of the iceberg. There are so many pastors offering this advice it could take down the Titanic. I looked back at the book *His Needs, Her Needs* by Willard F. Jr. Harley, a book I read while trying to sustain my first marriage. Two of the top men's needs are domestic support and admiration. Muffins and compliments, ladies. Some of the women's needs are honesty, and family commitment, which I'd think would go without saying for being married. Is commitment not standard anymore? Another need listed for women was conversation. Least our husbands grant us the privilege of their words.

Pastor John Piper is on video answering how a wife's submission should look. He responded that if the husband was "simply hurting her...she should endure verbal abuse for a season...and endure perhaps being smacked one night before seeking help from the church." In order to save her husband's soul.

Pastor Steven Cole says, "A Christian wife should live with a difficult husband so that he is attracted to Christ by her behavior." And "attractive behavior includes submission." He believes the Bible didn't just say to be submissive only to nice husbands. And I quote,

"So we must conclude that a wife may need to submit
to some abuse. The difficult question is, how much?"

How is this a difficult question? He did clarify that he means only verbal and emotional, not physical. But then he added that divorce for physical abuse isn't biblical, and a wife must not provoke her husband to anger but display a gentle spirit.

I see this kind of Biblical marriage all over the evangelical church. It's distorted at best, and formidably dishonest at worst, and I've been on the receiving end of it.

For all my time in the church, I was taught women's submission is a marker of a successful and happy Christian marriage. But if this is true, why is marriage failing so bad in the evangelical Christian church? Studies have shown marriage in the evangelical Christian church has the highest divorce rate compared to other denominations, perhaps because women are seen as unequal and under-authority of men. Which many churches might argue the last statement isn't true. But, the lack of women serving as pastors and elders and the collective silence on these issues by church influencers say otherwise.

It's no wonder the slogan Make America Great Again rang true for mostly the men. Bring back the time when women couldn't get a credit card without her husband's approval. If you are a woman reading this, when America was great, you weren't able to get a bank account, mortgage, or adopt a baby without a husband. You couldn't get birth control, and you'd have to leave your job if you got

114

pregnant. You couldn't become a lawyer or an astronaut or serve in combat. When Ruth Bader Ginsburg applied to Harvard Law School, the dean asked her to justify why she was taking up a man's spot. You couldn't serve on a jury or box in the Olympics or run in the Boston Marathon. You couldn't join a military academy. (Women now make up 38% of the Coast Guard Academy.) You couldn't complain if you were sexually harassed at work because it wasn't an offense. If your husband raped you, it was perfectly legal. If you wanted a divorce, you would have to prove a compelling reason why, and domestic violence wasn't considered compelling in many states.

Our country has a dark history of repressing women, and the church has both actively and passively enabled it. America was never great for women. At least not in the way it was for men. And unless more people speak up, it will continue to overflow into our churches, homes, and marriages.

Speaking up will always come at a cost. We will be met with resistance. Dr. Harriet Lerner recalled how much resistance came during her mother's lifetime when women were fighting for the right to vote.

> "The top experts in this society argued that to grant women the right to vote would rent asunder the entire fabric of democracy, and would bring about the downfall of the American family. This is the kind of resistance that we need to understand, and be prepared for that will happen, whether socially or in an intimate relationship when we make a truly substantive change."

I would add it's the same in church culture. When I've spoken out about women's issues or women's roles according to the church, I've come up against resistance every time, sold in a way to safeguard the church while silently preserving the patriarchy.

We finished the *Love and Respect* book study, and Jeff and I did walk away with a stronger marriage. Not from the book's advice, but from the conversations it sparked between us, allowing us to define how we wanted to paint our marriage, and what being a wife would mean for me, and downsizing the rest. Women are told not to focus on our pleasure but our spouses, causing women, not only in abusive situations but across the board to pause before speaking up for ourselves and to further neglect our own needs. It sets off a ripple effect of disconnectedness in our identity, our body, and our spirit, leaving us frantically searching outward for something to tell us what's wrong with us and how we can fix it stat. Enter all the self-help books.

15. Downsizing Grudges

"I could easily forgive his pride,
if he had not mortified mine."
Jane Austen, Pride and Prejudice.

After the book study ended, I couldn't shake the sense that something was off with my faith. I was embarrassed with the church's teachings on marital roles but dodged it by pretending everything was fine and consuming disproportionate amounts of frozen Thin Mints and reading every self-help book west of Seattle. All while still attending church, mind you. I knew I needed to speak out, but I couldn't see how that would look for me. I was having a hard enough time trying to belong. I didn't want to make waves by questioning. My goal was to fix myself so that I could recommence my previous pre-crisis church life.

It's fascinating how many self-help books, and I've read enough to last me to the second coming, center on forgiveness as a crucial part of moving forward in all areas of life, which made me feel good about myself because I'm pretty darn good at pardoning people. Except for about a dozen people I'll leave nameless because

I'm confident Jesus would agree they don't deserve it. Besides them, I'm good.

But still, I clutched a glass of milk and a generous stack of Girl Scout cookies and snuggled in tightly to the topic of forgiveness. As I read, my relationships with my siblings were the first to rise to the surface. My mom was barely sixteen, and my dad was nineteen when they tied the knot, still babies themselves. They promptly had four beautiful, healthy babies. Feeling societal pressure, that four was enough for such a young couple, my mom had her tubes tied, but they always wanted more children. Eight years after number four, my sister Christie was born, my mom had her tubes reversed. I owe my life to this decision because I am number five.

We became a family of six children with an age gap of eighteen years between us. Despite the age contrast, I have been close to each of my siblings at different times in varying ways. While we all love each other, we can each impressively hone our best school-yard-bully. I can never remember a time, ever, even to this very day, where there's been a lack of family drama among my siblings, making birthday parties and holidays like packing a room with unleashed hounds and feral cats. Anything could befall us.

In the thickets, after I filed for divorce, I was sad and unsettled. Talking with one of my older siblings, they handed me some unsolicited and rigid opinions furnished with a shade of superiority, in which I perceived immediately as judgment. I hated this. I hated being looked down on. With zero to be wasted in our heated discussion, I asked them, "Do you think you're better than me?"

Without hesitation, they replied, "Well, maybe. I'm doing better than you in my relationship and my finances. So, yeah, maybe."

I couldn't accept what I was hearing, and I rapidly shut myself off. Trying to recover from the divorce was hard enough. I retaliated and overlooked this sibling for years. Bitterness poured a concrete layer over my heart. I would sit in church, listening about forgiveness, and I tried. I prayed the prayers. I knew the Bible's rules. We should forgive seven times seventy because he who doesn't forgive, won't be forgiven.

I heard all the self-help variants. We forgive to free ourselves from the prison of resentment. It's a gift we give ourselves. It doesn't suggest reconciliation, and it's not declaring what they did was okay. It's not excusing it. It's not letting them off the hook or rejecting that it happened or living as a doormat. Oprah's forgiveness description was one of my favorites. She declares forgiveness is giving up the hope that the past could be any different.

I knew all of these ideas in my head, but my heart was holding out. Even though I decided to forgive, I seemed to have no command over my feelings. I appealed to God, saying I had forgiven them, and I wanted to be done with feelings of anger. Again and again, I prayed, but one mention of their name in passing and I would be steaming. And the cycle continued. Once more, I would say the encore prayer, but no matter how much I tried to feel better, the resentment lingered. I was carrying this now for a few years.

One afternoon while talking to my friend about the situation, I rambled on in my best Anne of Green Gables depths of despair. Then my friend asked me a question that changed everything.

"What would you need them to say for you to forgive? Both heart and mind?"

"Hmm, I don't know."

My friend had to end the call suddenly, and I was left thinking. And then it hit me.

The truth was that even if they got down on their hands and knees to sincerely apologize, I'd still be mad.

Realizing this was like being slapped in the head. There were too many thoughts racing through my mind. I hurriedly got off the phone.

Resentment. Animosity. They could have told me I was the best thing since Amazon Prime and offered the most earnest apology clothed in a hot Gucci clutch, and it would not have been sufficient. Maybe a Hermes Birkin bag. But probably not. If nothing they could say or do would make it right, the problem wasn't with them.

It was me.

I had spent years waxing and strengthening my story, allowing the narrative to grow like a Bonsai tree I was carefully nurturing and feeding and protecting. And this meant holding my walls high, my ego thick, and staying in a defensive state to avoid getting trampled. Because if by their calculations they were better, then I wasn't good enough as is and must do better at fixing, or at least concealing my flaws.

For too long, I affirmed this story as part of my identity. But now in one sweeping moment, by defining the stronghold of my not-enoughness, a switch flipped. The real blow wasn't that my sibling believed these things about me. *It was that I believed them about myself.*

I was warned Christians should steer clear of people like Marianne Williamson, so I immediately purchased her book *Return to Love*. On forgiveness, she says, "The decision to let go of our grievances against other people is the decision to see ourselves as we truly are because any darkness we let blind us to another's perfection also blinds us to our own." In the past, I struggled so hard but was unable to reach forgiveness in many situations. But after reading the book, it was a lightbulb moment for me to access forgiveness for myself and others. It came as a shock for me because I had gone to church my entire life, and it took the work of a "heretic" to show me a glimpse of God that would change my life.

I recognized how tough I was on myself, which reinforced the unrealistic expectations I elbowed on to others. When they fell short, I judged. They didn't get a pass. They were on the hook because I was on the hook. But I'm learning it's not my place to heap my expectations and standards on anybody. Forgiveness doesn't mean clearing them from my judgment. Forgiveness is understanding that it was never my job to judge them in the first place.

All the time I had spent praying to "feel" forgiveness was like McDreamy giving me a band-aid when I needed open-heart surgery. Forgiveness requires blood, sweat, and tears. It can be hard. It's not enough to say a prayer that we forgive those who've harmed us. That's just a mind game. It won't work. It's laboring over our thoughts, choosing to retire old expectations we've unfairly placed on people and birth something new. Relationships are inherently hard, on purpose. They challenge us to love better and to accept others as they are, not just when they fit our expectations.

One of my favorite authors, Anne Lamott, talked once about the process of writing a story. She said many authors write the plot. They lay out the story from start to finish. Then, only after the plot has been written, they whip up the characters to fit into it. She teaches to do the opposite. That we should commit ourselves to the characters first, not the story plot. It's an important life principle. Most often, I create a storyline of my plans, all meticulously thought out, and then I expect others to fall into line with my plot. Because why shouldn't they? It's a good storyline. For me.

But when they don't fall into step, it's easy to stop writing them into my story. It creates almost this robotic dynamic of life. Controlling life and not living or let live. What if I let people be who they are? Exactly where they are? Without changing them or trying to spin them into my story? What if I acknowledged they also held a pen and are beautifully writing their own story too?

It would considerably ease much of the pressure I feel. I wouldn't be angry, frustrated, or sad at the things they do. That's part of their story, not mine. I wouldn't fear their story not molding into mine. I would take charge of my story, and only my story, and still love their story, for them. Embracing someone only when they fit into my story is control, not love. Committing to the characters, not the story, frees us to fall in love with people. It might be the most important thing I'm learning. To let go and love without qualification. To forgive, both them and myself. Because if we can't forgive, can we truly love?

Nelson Mandela might be the most inspiring example of forgiveness. After being wrongly in prison in South Africa for twenty-seven years, he wrote, "Forgiveness liberates the soul, it removes fear. That's why it's such a powerful weapon." Years ago, I watched a documentary where he returned to the very cell he lived in during most of his prison stay. He said if he didn't forgive the people who had persecuted him, it would be like putting himself back in that cell.

Forgiveness is the hardest when we don't know how to practice it with ourselves first. The people in my life who seem to be most reluctant to forgive and judge others with the most biased, are so incredibly tough on themselves. I see this in myself and other women, and it's particularly strong with those who've been in an abusive relationship. Women who have been told they were not good enough so many times, they have adopted it as their own thoughts. Withholding forgiveness is heavy and oppressive. It impresses on everything we say, everything we do. Directly or indirectly, it always leaves a mark.

Being able to forgive is a stepping stone to living free. Learning to let go of mistakes opens the floodgates to fully loving who we are. Forgiveness is letting go of our old expectations for ourselves and others, accepting life didn't happen that way, but it happened the way it was supposed to. The only choice we have is how we respond with love or hate. And in our response is a new beginning to our story.

16. Zumba Church

It was only with this new lightness of forgiveness, in the space of love and openness, that I began to examine my increasing uncertainty in the church. I never doubted God, but I was moderately sure some of God's main people were fronting a hidden agenda. I grappled with the church's stance on marriage and women's roles. At this point, I couldn't talk to anyone about my thoughts. Most of my friends were church people, and they didn't understand. So I did the next best thing and tried to find a book by someone who has experienced this. After combing dozens of Christian living books, nothing was chiming true. Then I found Rachel Held Evans.

I poured through her book, *Evolving in Monkey Town: How a Girl Who Knew All the Answers Learned to Ask the Questions*. In these pages, I found a sanctuary of honesty of her struggles and doubts with church theology, some of the same challenges I was muddling through. The story that stayed with me most is when Rachel stumbled upon a documentary about women's oppression in Afghanistan before the US invaded the country. The documentary, *Behind the Veil*, showed a woman named Zarmina accused of murdering her abusive husband. She was beaten for two days with steel cables until she confessed, then imprisoned in Afghan for three years. Her oldest daughters were sold into sex slavery by relatives. After all her suffering, they dragged her into an arena, and, with an audience of nearly thirty thousand people watching, she was flanked and then shot dead. Realizing that Zarmina was unsaved by evangelical standards, Rachel talked about her anger with God and the questions she had in the fallout of viewing the documentary.

> "Suddenly abstract concepts about heaven and hell, election, and free will, religious pluralism and exclusivism had a name: Zarmina. I felt like I could come to terms with Zarmina's suffering if it were restricted to this lifetime, if I knew that God would grant her some sort of justice after death. But the idea that this woman passed from agony to agony, from torture to torture, from a lifetime of pain and sadness to an eternity of pain and sadness, all because she had less information about the gospel than I did, seemed cruel, even sadistic." (Page 99).

This story grieved me. Did I believe Zarmina was going to hell? My first thought was surely not. But that couldn't be right. It didn't line up with what I learned in the evangelical church. If she hadn't said the prayer, accepting Jesus as her personal savior, then she couldn't be in heaven. Nope. No. This could not be from a loving God. And then immediately, this rule I had carried for years dissipated. I didn't believe it anymore. I didn't become angry with God. I still felt practically, and idealistically God was loving. But I was tied in knots with the church's viewpoints and overtaken with discouragement. I was not willing to accept my relationship with the church as irreparable. I wondered how far we have drifted from what a loving God means. I wanted to get back to God as love and loving.

124

I found a popular book on the church circuit, Crazy Love by popular pastor Francis Chan: *Overwhelmed by a Relentless God*. In the description I read, "God is love. Crazy, relentless, all-powerful love. Have you ever wondered if we're missing it?" Well, yes, actually, I did wonder. And so with the optimism of finding this declared "authentic faith that addresses the problems of our world with tangible, even radical, solutions," I cracked open the cover. I was ready to be inspired by genuine Godly love, but the words left me more discouraged than before. Here I was reading a book about crazy God love, and I felt even more turned off than before. What was wrong with me? One morning while power walking with a friend, I told her, "I'm just not relating to it." She reminded me that not all books are for everyone, and I agreed. I appreciated having someone to talk to about it, but here I was. Again. Another book seemingly the entire Christian community embraced, quoted, and studied, and I was unresponsive, maybe even annoyed by it. I was torn. Francis Chan is so esteemed in the church. I must not be understanding it. That night I gave it one more shot. I started over in case I had missed something, and it wasn't long before I read:

"Because God hates sin, He has to punish those guilty of sin. Maybe that's not an appealing standard. But to put it bluntly, when you get your own universe, you can make your own standards. When we disagree, agree, let's not assume it's His reasoning that needs correction." (Page 36).

Unbending. Uncaring. Lacking compassion. All presented as the way God loves us. I waved the book off.

I visited the moms' group from the movie-theater church. I loved going because it was two prized hours to sip coffee and talk with people who didn't want milk from the fountain of my breast. I met the most amazing women, like Danielle, who's realness left me in

125

awe. Or Amber, an outgoing, gorgeous mom of four who allowed me to cry on her shoulder when I was exhausted or messing up or couldn't get Evan to nap. On numerous occasions, she gave me the best parenting advice, backed up with crazy stories that would have me in fits of laughter, and always put my failings in perspective. The whole mom's group was giddy because the IF:Gathering was coming up. It was a Christian women's conference in Austin, and it sold out within minutes. But for women and churches all over the globe who couldn't come to Austin, or didn't get a ticket, it was offered as a live stream. You could watch from home, but many watched at small gatherings at their local church, which is what we were doing. Word on the street was a bunch of the Christian women leaders were tired of speaking at conferences they themselves wouldn't want to attend, so they decided to formulate a conference directed at the new generation. They said it was going to be different, and I was looking forward to attending.

I had heard there would be diversity in the speakers to serve the various viewpoints and many denominations in Christianity. A conference for all. I desperately welcomed it, because, at this point, I was seriously working to hide the feeling I didn't belong anywhere in the church. I felt a kinship at the conference when I heard Sarah Bessey speak. She said she was too conservative for the liberals and too liberal for the conservatives. This I could relate to. I found her book *Jesus Feminist* and later, when she announced *Out of Sorts: Making Peace with an Evolving Faith*, I pre-ordered and waited eagerly.

She writes:

"A lot of people in my generation might be giving up on Church, but there are a lot of us returning, redefining, reclaiming Church too. We aren't foolish or blind or unconcerned or uneducated or unthinking. We have weighed our choices, more than anyone will know. We are choosing this and we will keep choosing each other. And sometimes our way of understanding or "doing" church looks very different, but we're still here. I know some of us are meant to go, some are meant to stay, and most of us do a bit of both in a lifetime." (Page 96).

I wanted to redefine what church was for me, but I had no idea how or what that would look like. I began skipping church both decisively and a bit unconsciously. I was dodging the feeling of being lost, left out, and disconnected. Instead, I laced up my sneakers, pulled my too-tight yoga pants over my muffin top, and rolled the baby stroller right into Zumba class. The quietness of a church service would provoke the baby to cry, but in Zumba, the intense African-Latin vibrations kept him sound asleep while I danced around.

I looked foolish, I'm sure of it, but I didn't care one bit, even when there was twerking. A lot of twerking. I thought it would be the twerking that did me in. My twerking looked less like Miley Cyrus sexy dancing and more like Zach Galifianakis choking on a Java Chip Frappuccino. But it wasn't the twerking that nearly killed me. It was pivoting. During one class, I was dancing around, and I tried to do a pivot spin, but the grip on my shoes was too much. I couldn't freely spin or correct directions without nearly wrenching my knee. I went home and searched the internet, only to unearth the most fantastic thing, unique Zumba socks that slipped over my shoes and made pivoting easier.

I loved Zumba and saw the same women nearly every week. They were all shapes, sizes, and nationalities. Some didn't speak English, but it didn't even matter. We were unspoken friends who cha-cha'd and shook our butts and danced together. I couldn't explain why sometimes leaving a church service, I would feel depressed and out of place and helpless to freely search for God. But when I left Zumba, I felt connected to new life running the course of my body.

Surely it was blood flow from the twerking. But also, it was natural too. Zumba became my church.

I let myself imagine what if the church was more like Zumba? Maybe our tagline would be like the one I read in class, "Ditch the Workout, Join the Party." And most definitely, my Zumba church would hand out the unique socks, freeing people to pivot as they needed. It would be high intensity but lower if you're tired. We would come precisely how we were and dance our hearts out, wholly aware but not caring how awkward we looked. We would build our strengths and increase our flexibility because this is what church should be.

Note: Rachel Held Evans passed away in the midst of me writing this book. She left behind two small children and a husband. Although she was young, her work touched thousands of lives, including mine. I am forever grateful.

17. Downsizing Restaurant Prayer

Most nights, I would carry my blossoming hostility towards the church to the foot of our California king, kneel, and pray about it. All the church advice pointed this way. Give it to God. Let Go and Let God. Leave it at His feet. Except everything I knew of prayer was falling apart. The significant parts but also the nuances too.

Born-agains learn to kneel at the foot of the bed, hands folded, head bowed. At the end of the prayer, you say Amen or in long-form, In Jesus' name, Amen. Or Ahmen if you're fancy. Some pray to God or Lord or Heavenly Father. I don't use the word, Lord. I think of War Lords and Drug Lords and Lord of the Rings and also Game of Thrones. I've never seen Game of Thrones, but in my mind's eye, they have Lords. I've heard you're not supposed to pray to Jesus, but this was after I'd already developed the bad habit. But I guess it's not as bad as the Catholics who pray to Mary and, according to Christians, don't know they can go straight to the source. I've never prayed to Mary, but I can see why it's inviting. Some things are just more natural said to a consoling and earnest mother. I think the real spoil is when people pray to Daddy or Papa. I always

129

picture The Notorious B.I.G. rapping, "I love it when you call me big pop-pa." It's all very righteous.

Then, there are the unspoken prayer rules I grew up with, like praying at every meal. I know many families who practice this, even when at restaurants. Restaurant prayer is tricky. Timing is critical. It's after the server drops the food, but quickly before she returns with extra napkins and ketchup.

I heard a pastor bait the congregation, "God sees if you're too timid in your faith to pray in restaurants."

I find most restaurant prayer is too goody-goody for me. A way to broadcast to everyone you're a Christian, and you aren't embarrassed to thank God for these crinkle-cut sweet potato fries, lest they be blessed. But didn't Jesus most often go to desolate places to pray alone?

I do love that when our extended family is together at Thanksgiving, before we carve the turkey, we circle the kitchen, hold hands, and my Uncle Greg prays. He loves God, and he's also known for his many words. The running joke is that our real prayer is hoping he finishes before Christmas.

I hear people define prayer as the way we communicate with God. People say they talk to God, and he talks back. Like a conversation. I struggle to understand this because it feels too irreverent to me, to humanize the Almighty Creator of the universe to my chit chat buddy.

Have you ever looked up your name's meaning? My name, Angela, means a messenger of God. I've never believed it because I don't hear God the same way my friends listen to Him (or Her). In church, people say things like, "God told me to do this" or my favorite, "God told me to tell you…". I've clearly pissed God off with my laziness or love of pop culture, or maybe he's disappointed because I secretly want to be a burlesque dancer with cherry red lips and precariously placed tassels. Because God doesn't talk to me the way he seems to talk to others. I sit quietly with my prayers and look up to the sky and wait. And nothing happens. And nothing happens so often I've given up expecting a response. But it hasn't stopped me from praying.

In the praying moments, I'm like an exhausted, famine farmer who's just planted the last damn seeds he has in a waterless field, glaring at the ground, and nothing is happening. But when I look back at my life, I see prayers answered the same way you'd watch the farmer's field sprout in a time-lapse video. Over time the things I'd misunderstood and underestimated, like heartbreak and failed dreams, have transformed to lush flower beds and fruit trees. I have no doubt I'll always have weeds in my garden, but also no doubt God was with me. So I keep praying.

I pray for healing and finances and relationships and coveted parking spaces when shopping on Black Friday, all asking God to be of service to me. I've heard pastors say that God cares about every little thing we have to say. Even the parking spaces. Ask, and you'll be given. It's all very self-centered, yet holy.

I see prayer meetings and prayer chains and prayer closets. I like the idea of clearing aside shoes and old winter jackets to have a consecrated spot to talk to God or hide from my family. A nice change of scenery from when I say I'm using the bathroom, but really, I'm scrolling *Facebook*.

Listening to others pray out loud sometimes makes me uncomfortable. I guess it depends on how they say it. Sometimes, it can be so contrived. A little too planned and almost manipulative. An assertion of what we think other people need to hear disguised as our prayer. Kind of like when the pastor makes a good point, and you are elbowing your husband to make sure he knows the messianic message was meant for him. One time at a women's bible study, the women were chatting loudly and ignoring the leader trying to quiet the room. She prayed for God to "quiet the women's spirits." It was the most graceful way I've ever heard anyone tell a group to shut up. I was impressed.

One of my best friends often asks if she can pray over me. I want to say no, but because I adore her, I concede, but I find it awkward because the way she prays is not the way I talk to God. I'm working on seeing it as loving and a devout expression for her. I never know what to say at the end, so I say thank you.

What is wrong with me? Will I ever get to a place where I appreciate the communal prayer as something beautiful even though it's not my way? Will I remain jaded at the way prayer often includes interjected absolutes I don't agree with? I don't know. I just don't know.

18. Downsizing Unspoken Rules

One of my husband's duties in the Coast Guard is helping organize search and rescue cases in our area. This requires calls at all hours of the night. If I'm honest, I'm usually annoyed and somewhat pissy when the phone rings at 2:00 am after I've laid Ethan to sleep for the third time and because my husband can't whisper. He just can't. And then I hear the calls and feel lousy because it's usually boats capsizing and people drowning or lost at sea. One night a teenage boy was hiking near a cliff when he fell and landed right on a dirt ledge maybe two feet wide and two hundred feet above the water. He stood on the side of a cliff, hanging on for dear life. One tiny move on his part or any crumbling of dirt under his feet spelled certain death. I can't imagine what the minutes were like waiting for the Coast Guard rescuers. I think he stood there for an hour before a rescue swimmer was dropped on a 200-foot cable to pluck him off the cliff and bring him to safety.

This responsibility my husband has in the Coast Guard is called Search and Rescue Mission Coordinator or SMC because acronyms and the military are BFFs. I adopted this acronym for my Spiritual Midlife Crisis because I feel I'm on my own search and rescue mission. At times I feel like I'm living in a dream, waiting for my rescue. I am dangling off a cliff with dirt crumbling under my feet. I wait and then wait some more. I'm weak, and things shift into a mirage. In the horizon, I see the helicopter coming to save me. God is lowered on a rescue wire and shovels me up. Together we are pulled back up towards the helicopter cabin, and we fall inside. And then the craziest thing happens. The pilot looks back, and it's me. I'm not just the one being rescued, but I'm also the navigator. Maybe the only reason God could get to me was that I'd directed the path allowing the rescue.

One of the hardest things about going through an SMC is trying to talk about it. Many discussions have left me more perplexed and lost as I've sought to explain what I'm going through. I typically get two responses. One, it makes people feel uncomfortable that I would question the church. Or two, it makes people feel empowered because they have the perfect answer for my questioning.

At lunch one afternoon, I tried talking with my friend Maxine about my struggles with the church. She looked at me reluctantly. It was clear she didn't understand. I thought it was my fault because I didn't explain it well enough, so I continued to clarify further, but I only seemed to stuff my foot further down my throat. She smiled politely and a little anxiously and told me she didn't want to focus on the negatives because she loved the Christian church and was uncomfortable "bad mouthing" the church. And then I realized it wasn't that I couldn't articulate the issue, it was that she could not or did not want to hear it. She is beautiful and smart. She would give me the shirt off her back. She'd bring me a meal when I was sick or watch my babies. But she couldn't go there with me. I tried not to take it personally, but I did. I felt unseen and dismissed.

This wasn't a solo incident. At times I've made comments about something I'm questioning in the church, and I see people visibly tense up and become quiet or make a declaration about their loyalty to the church. Sometimes people will listen sympathetically but then respond with what I read as pity.

I've had two friends tell me, "I'm sorry you had a bad encounter with the church." Emphasis on you. Herein lies the problem. They viewed it as my issue and not a collective problem of the church. And to be clear, this *is* my issue. But it's not only mine. The church has injured thousands of women in the same way. Acknowledging it has happened and is still happening, isn't saying you think everyone in the church is terrible and sexist. But it allows Christians a chance to make real change. Because it's not just my issue, it belongs to everyone.

I heard someone say, "I don't need to be concerned about the person peeing into the pool because I'm on the other end."

Or more eloquently put by Martin Luther King Jr. "An injustice anywhere is a threat to justice everywhere." And I think this applies to the church because if we are considered one body, then a broken hand prevents us from reaching out. A broken foot prevents us from walking in love. A spine out of alignment prevents us from walking tall. And when you have an alignment issue, you don't ignore it. You get an adjustment.

The other response I get to my SMC is a fix-it attempt from people who feel warranted to tell me the solutions to all my questions. They believe questioning the church stems from a wavering faith or shaky foundation. I've taken a few people up on trying to fix me because I must be broken and want to be fixed, and, yes, please glue me back together. Being in this crisis place has majorly sucked. My life would be more comfortable if I could go back to a time before all this chaos, but tragically it doesn't work like that.

The people who were wholeheartedly offering to help me could not understand the place I was in. They would answer my questions with clichés and typical Christian talking points, the ones I knew word-for-word. I couldn't accept the answers at face value anymore. The people trying to help me had never been in a position where they felt the need to question the church, and most were taught it was dangerous to inquire about things already deemed answered. Some would say, "Ask all the questions because God is bigger than our questions. God can handle it." But the unspoken rule is only to ask God questions the church hasn't already decided on.

For many, questioning the church doctrine means questioning God, and therefore questioning the very foundation of faith. For those who were taught that people who don't believe in Jesus, are going to burn eternally in hell, well, this makes the act of questioning treacherous. For them, a lot is riding on being sure. In fact, everything is riding on being sure.

I understand. It's what I learned, and that's why being in an SMC is such a scary place. I tried to be gracious because not too long ago, I was there, well-meaning and trying to save lost friends from backsliding and hell and Beyoncé songs. I know they mean well and I decided to be kind when they offered this. Sometimes in my exhaustion, I've been anything but. I've been guarded, disappointed, and critical. But I couldn't take advice from people who hadn't even taken a bus through this land, let alone stop for a full visit. I equated it to a pacifist trying to give an Army commander strategies on combat. You have no idea how to fight unless you've been in the trenches. I tried to find people who had experienced an SMC.

I looked for those Brené Brown says are in the arena. The ones Theodore Roosevelt was talking about when he said,

> "It is not the critic who counts; not the man who points out how the strong man stumbles, or where the doer of deeds could have done them better. The credit belongs to the man who is actually in the arena, whose face is marred by dust and sweat and blood; who strives valiantly; who errs, who comes short again and again, because there is no effort without

error and shortcoming; but who does actually strive to do the deeds; who knows great enthusiasms, the great devotions; who spends himself in a worthy cause; who at the best knows in the end the triumph of high achievement, and who at the worst, if he fails, at least fails while daring greatly, so that his place shall never be with those cold and timid souls who neither know victory nor defeat."

I forgot there is a third response from well-meaning people. I'm not sure how I forgot this because it's genuinely a church classic. There have been times I'll mention issues about scripture being misrepresented or taught in ways that are damaging towards women, and it's met with a dismissive, "Well, the church is run by sinners" — followed by something easy like, "Broken people in a broken world." A get-over-it mentality. Agreed, the church is run by imperfect people. But this does not mean our church leaders and members get a pass to ignore deeply rooted troubles and a moral duty to do better.

I struggled with each type of these responses in different ways, and my inability to connect with my church friends or have them at least understand why I was frustrated, pushed me further into unconnectedness and exhaustion. I felt guilty that my story, or the way I was telling it, was making people uncomfortable, and I wondered if there was a better way to talk about all this.

I enrolled in *The Wisdom of Story*, a workshop with Glennon Doyle & Brené Brown, exploring how to find the wisdom in our stories and telling them with honesty and courage. The question was posed, "What are the rules currently in place in your world? What are the spoken or unspoken messages and expectations that are part of your family, community, or culture?" Without hesitation, I recognized a clear rule for me as a churchgoer was to hold the church in a good light. People's salvation depends on this. Deviate from this, and things fall apart. The act of noticing this unspoken rule allowed me to see it wasn't right. It is not now, nor has it ever been, my job to hold the church in a good light. I had spent too much time in my first marriage trying to put lipstick on a pig and paint something broken in a good light, and I was done. The entire Christian structure doesn't rest on me making people feel good about the church. My questioning will not send people to hell. I do not carry that power. I also realized it's not my job to make others comfortable. It's their job. I'm responsible for being loving, but I cannot continue to take on the absurd occupation of managing everyone else's feelings, responses, and thoughts. Doing this for myself is a full-time job. Knowing what, and who, I value and what all of this looks like for me and mine - that's my work. Some people won't think it's loving. And that's okay. More on this later.

What is my job is to show up with dignity, to tell my truth, not to make it look pretty, not to inflate it or decrease it. It is my job to embrace the pain and learn from it. It's my job to own my story and learn how I want it to be told.

I've given much thought to this. How do I want my story to be told? What do I want the ending to be? I learned it's essential to feel the pain and process it, so I don't pass our hurt on to others. And also that we should share our stories only when they are scars and not open wounds. And Brené says share only with people who have earned the right to hear it. Many of the people weighing in on my situation, didn't have the right to chime in, but it didn't stop them from doing it, or me for allowing it. They would offer up their thoughts, and like tiny hotel shampoo bottles, I had no use for them, but I still took them home.

In my searching, I so badly wanted to connect to someone who had been in my shoes, but in my desperation, I wasn't qualifying the conversations I was having. In the audiobook *The Dance of Connection*, I heard Harriet Lerner discusses the challenges of intimacy in women's relationships.

She says:

"I don't believe it's a great idea when it comes to truth-telling about difficult issues to just shut our eyes, hold our noses and jump, which is what most of us do. Sometimes truth-telling, like peacemaking, has to be slowly worked towards. Plotted, strategized, and planned so that we can lay the groundwork for people to be able to listen to each other or even to stay in the same room. I used to think that timing and tack are the opposite of honesty and now I believe timing and tack are exactly what makes honesty possible with the most difficult people and in the most difficult of circumstances."

Over many failed conversations, and a few lost friendships, I learned you couldn't have a genuine conversation where there is fear. And there's a lot of fear when talking about the church and God — trying to share with those you love that you are struggling spiritually, relationally, or any important life juncture situation is hard. Most of our people love us always, but they like us just the way we are. They don't want us to change. Most people fear change. And when I started sharing my doubts and questions with others, they felt like I was questioning their choices and values.

I set a few goals. To be more intentional about if, and when, I would engage in a conversation, especially when the stakes seemed higher. To come to the conversation lightly and maintain self-awareness. To notice if they looked angry or frustrated or defeated. I've felt all of these, and it never leads to understanding. To let go of any expectations on them, and only put an expectation on how I show up. To release any pressure on the outcome. To own responsibility for my feelings but not theirs. Even when it feels like I don't have a choice, I try to remember; I always have a choice in how I show up. When the conversation starts to feel too powerful, it's usually because I'm telling myself something significant is riding on gaining this person's understanding, validation, or respect. But 99% of the time this is not true. Most of the time nothing is genuinely at stake at the moment. If they don't understand, it's okay. We can take a breath and try again. Or not. We don't need to solve and agree and tie everything up in a neat little Kate Spade bow. Some religious leaders have attempted this, and it hasn't worked out so well.

19. More Thoughts on Prayer

Trying to cook dinner while toddlers run at your feet is crazy-making. I've burned my hand and nearly chopped off a finger trying to feed my family. The Bible says Jesus gave thanks before feeding the multitudes, and I sometimes wonder if he was often rushing too because, in the midst of giving us a few guidelines on prayer, he left out a few things. Like how long should prayer be for top effectiveness? Why would Jesus say not to babble when praying because the Bible says, "God knows our needs before we ask Him," and follows with "to pray without ceasing"? And what is the proper prayer ratio for talking versus listening? Then I would ask what he meant by confessing our sins. It must be important because Stephen Colbert devotes an entire segment of his show for his Midnight Confessions. Once he started with the disclaimer, "I don't know if these are technically sins, but I do feel bad about them." Which I think is where most of us are.

I've never been to confession, but once while I was visiting a basilica, I was tempted to try. Unfortunately, the line was too long. There were four confessional boxes, but only one priest was working. If this were a Home Depot, they would, for sure, add another checker. The church should consider this. Or even a self-checkout where we hold up our iPhones to a church kiosk that scans our internet history, a much faster way to guilt us. Although confession gets a bad rap for being shame-inducing, if done right, it can be a healing experience, because it's not the stories and photos we freely share on social media but the ones we keep hidden and nameless that weigh us down the most. Confession shines a light and assigns a name and makes us more perfectly-imperfect and human in a world where people are trying to be anything else.

During church prayer, my mind wanders. Sometimes it's because I lack the ability to sit still, or sometimes it's because of the pastor's directions. If I had a nickel for every time I heard, "Now with eyes closed and nobody looking around, raise your hand if...." God forgive them if they don't give us instructions on what to do with our bodies. We would look around frantically, wondering if we should sit or stand or kneel. If we should keep our eyes open or shut. Hands together or outstretched. If you're wondering, the answer is always outstretched.

When I was little, we attended one church they labeled Pentecostal. If you've been to a Pentecostal church, you've likely heard people praying in tongues. It's considered a special gift from God, where someone cries out a prayer in odd, loud sounds. It's incomprehensible to everyone. Then God will assign someone else in the room the key to this cryptic yelling prayer. That person would be able to translate, in real words, for all the rest of us to understand. It's quite scary, and as a little girl, I remember praying, *Dear God, please never, ever give me that gift.*

Sometimes when I need help, I feel bad asking God to come to help me. Because of Haiti and world hunger and the Sarah

McLachlan puppies. God is busy and likely out there roaming the world, trying to fix everyone's problems, and I shouldn't bother the Creator with mine. It makes me wonder, where is God when not with me? After the 2016 election, Franklin Graham preached about how Donald Trump was made President because "God showed up." Which is to imply God was somewhere else during the campaigning and likely missed hearing about all the pussy-grabbing, Russian meetings, and email servers. What makes God show up? I think our views on prayer are the most telling of how we view God's abilities, God's heart, and where God usually is, on a day-to-day, hour-to-hour, minute-by-minute account.

I've seen Christians write in prayer journals and mark off prayers God answers for them. They believe their prayers prompt God to move. Why does God only answer some prayers and not others? Does God choose to heal people based on how hard people pray for them? Or how many? A few years ago, my dad was diagnosed with stage four lung cancer. At the same time, my beloved, beautiful Auntie Doris was also given a diagnosis of stage four lung cancer. My whole family prayed for them both. A few months later, my Auntie passed. We were devastated. Did my family not pray hard enough for her? What is the tipping point of prayer? Jesus said where two or three gather in my name, there am I with them. So is God not with me when I'm alone? How many people are necessary to incite God to heal? When people ask in a *Facebook* status for prayer, and others reply with the folded hands emoji, does that help? What if only one or two people comment?

There are two ways this can go. Either God is not a loving God, because why spare some and not others, or I was taught a distorted view of God and prayer. Bible scholar and Episcopal Bishop John Shelby Spong wrote about an experience that shaped his understanding of prayer. He was called to the hospital to visit a young, non-religious, mom of three. When he arrived, he learned she had a terminal diagnosis. Knowing her time was limited, they jumped right into deep conversations about grief, fears, and anger. They talked about her sadness, knowing she wouldn't see her three children grow up and connected meaningfully in a way only looming death will bring. When it was time for him to leave, he shifted into his ordained capacity and felt he should pray, because that's what pastors do. It was a general prayer that strung together one cliché after another. When he finished, he felt diminished by the prayer and thought she did too. When he compared the hours they spent sharing grief and all the emotions versus the departing prayer, he noticed one expanded life by opening a relationship, and the other seemed to close it. It made him ask, which one was the real prayer?

This story hit home for me. I've come to see prayer as not something to be done but a way of living, the part that says pray without ceasing. How would we live differently if we believed our whole lives are the prayer? And prayer doesn't need to be words. Years ago, I worked with a client who had been married for 40 years and living the retired dream, traveling everywhere with her husband. She would bring in photos of their trek across Europe and cruise to Alaska, and they seemed so happy together. One day she nearly crawled in with an air of sadness so palpable you could reach your hand up and touch it. She announced her husband had left her for her best friend. Over the next few weeks, her appearance completely changed. She fell into a depression, and amid her darkest moment, I had no clue what to say to her. I was young and wet behind the ears.

I asked a wise friend, "What can I possibly say to her?"

Her reply was so profound and straightforward for me at that moment. "You don't say anything, you cry with her."

This is a living prayer. The kind that says we aren't alone. We have people walking alongside us, and not being alone is one of the most treasured gifts we can give. It breathes hope and love. This is God.

The idea of prayer as a way of being in the world, explains why I sometimes don't have the words for praying, but I know I need it. I feel empty. Unsure. A little desperate. Bob Cornwall wrote, "I see prayer as our creative and affirmative desire to be in alignment with and embody God's vision for our lives and the world around us."

Prayer can be books, poetry, and music. Prayer is cooking and writing, and when after 32 hours of labor, they placed my beautiful baby on my chest. It's watching the ocean and rainbows and sun and moon and stars and laying in my husband's arms after making love. Prayer is time with family and friends and even more so with my enemies. Why does God answer some prayers and not others? God doesn't. Prayer is about transportation and transformation. Ours. Not Gods. God isn't sitting somewhere else on a cloud deciding who's prayers to grant. Prayer is less a thing to do, but something to be experienced. To be changed. To transcend. People say to pray is to seek the face of God, but I think to pray is to be the face of God.

How long should a prayer be? A lifetime.

20. Downsizing Fossils and Fox

Right out of high school, I attended a local Baptist university. On-campus was Wanda's Place, a popular cafe for students to grab a bite. In between my classes, I would stop there for a sugary drink. To feel better about myself, and since it did have a shot of espresso, I called it coffee. It was typical to see, in the corner of the cafe, a group of students meeting for a bible study. Sounds from the television's news commentary always filled the room. Likely some Fox News anchor, maybe Glen Beck monologuing about how the country was in imminent danger of a natural disaster and conveniently selling survival kits. Or maybe it was Bill O'Reilly. After all, this was before him, and Roger Ailes, CEO of Fox News, left the network following multiple sexual harassment accusations. But either way, it was perpetually on Fox News. Never CNN and most definitely not MSNBC. Not even local news. Exclusively Fox. Perhaps this was to directly counter the worldly ideas promoted at secular, liberal-leaning colleges, but nonetheless, the message was clear. Christians are Republicans. It was a political life sentence issued with my salvation and had already been determined for me. I wonder if, over a decade later, they still exclusively show Fox News. I wonder if everything has changed, or just me?

In my political science classes, we had to debate a controversial topic. Only there was never any real controversy. We were a yes-man kind of group. At this time, stem cell research was the political issue sweeping the Christian world. One gal stood up and presented an argument against altering cells of the unborn even if the purpose was to save the life of the mother, the life of the baby, or prevent a major disability.

"God loves us and made us just the way we are." she declared. "We shouldn't change God's work." She affirmed what a blessing children with disabilities are.

The class applauded her. I couldn't. First, I agreed with her, a thousand over. Children with disabilities are no less of a blessing or beauty. They are. But I don't believe we have to directly equate the blessing and value of the disabled with a doctor's abilities to heal illnesses, disability, or even death when preventable.

But nobody was saying it. All of a sudden, the room felt hot. I twisted my hands open and slowly raised one. She called on me.

"I'm going to play devil's advocate, okay?"

She grinned with a nod.

"If your baby was born with a cleft lip, knowing that nursing and other life functions would be more challenging for her, would you get it fixed after she was born?"

Half smiling now, she considered it. "Yes."

"Then, why is it morally wrong to do it before they are born?"

Silence.

Seconds later, the instructor interrupted to announce it was a good time to stop, and he dismissed the class. But it stayed with me. It wasn't that specific topic, but the perpetual head nodding by my peers and the disapproval of pushback as if questioning the issues was questioning the existence of God.

Jeff and I had now been living in Washington state for almost a year when I bought a plane ticket to see my parents in Southern California. I felt lucky because Evan was still under two years old, which meant I only needed to buy one ticket. I packed light, just a full backpack, and didn't bring a stroller because my mom had one for when we landed. As Jeff drove us to the airport, we hit bumper-to-bumper traffic and finally arrived 45 minutes before my flight was boarding. The TSA line wrapped around the airport with many frustrated people. Including Evan. He whined and wanted down, and the line was not budging. He cried, and people looked at us with growing irritation. An older woman looked at me with compassion as I shifted Evan around. She asked how old he was and made small talk with me. I told her we were likely going to miss our flight because the line was moving at a snail's pace.

She said, "Nope." And then immediately commanded the attention of the room, coordinating people to get me to the front. She never said what she did for her career, but I just knew she was a high school teacher. I would bet money on it because nobody can command a room like a high school teacher.

Time was ticking. After my body scan, with Evan in a baby carrier on my front, and a weighty backpack bouncing on my rear, I ran. I ran like Melissa McCarthy runs from Jason Bateman. Sadly, the airport was just too big, and I missed the flight by five minutes. I stood there totally sweaty from all my crazy mom hormones and my jog across the airport, as the attendant searched for a new flight for us. Evan was rolling around the less-than-sterile floor like a maniac. I was confused when she informed me the next flight was in seven hours.

"Seven hours?" I gasped.

She nonchalantly kept typing then looked up. "Well?"

"I don't understand. There has to be something else?" I silently cursed her. And TSA. And traffic. And myself, for not leaving with enough time to spare.

"Sorry," she said apathetically.

I pointed at my kid, who was now pushing all the elevator buttons. "Just what am I supposed to do with him for seven hours in an airport?" I knew this wasn't her problem, but at the moment everything was fuzzy.

She shrugged her shoulders.

"Fine. I'll take it."

"Perfect! Let me get your new ticket printed."

I called Jeff and cried, but he was working and couldn't come back. He suggested I wait at the USO lounge. The USO is a non-profit organization that offers services to the military, including hosting lounges at several airports for military members and their families to rest while waiting for flights. A few years back, I volunteered at the USO to fill packages for the troops overseas, but I had no idea about the airport lounges.

I hesitated because going to the USO would mean leaving the main area and then coming back through the bloody TSA line again. I looked over at Evan, who was inching around the dirty airport floor climbing under people's seats and pushing their luggage over. I knew I wouldn't survive this for seven hours, and reluctantly left the main area and headed to the lounge. As I slogged into the USO, I was greeted by a friendly teenage girl who was volunteering with her dad. They were both so welcoming. They stored my luggage and fed us lunch. The USO had toys and books and Mickey Mouse showing in the kids' room. Hello, they had a kid's room! While I ate lunch, the teen volunteer played and chased Evan up and down the hall. The thought that people take precious time from their days to battle traffic and then airport parking, all in supporting the military, is so heartwarming. The USO volunteers have my deepest gratitude.

We made it to my parents, and my mom took over with Evan. My family decided to try something touristy and settled on the La Brea Tar Pits in Los Angeles, a popular site where fossils of mammoths and saber-toothed tigers were found. I had been once when I was little but had no memory of it. Growing up in a Christian high school, we were taught Creationism and also a healthy amount of disdain for atheists, even the ones who wear the "local friendly atheist" shirts. Friendly and atheist in the same sentence was a fallacy, just like evolution. In my early teens, I read one of Pastor John Hagee's books. I'm not sure if it was *The Beginning of the End* or *From Daniel to Doomsday*, but if the titles don't tell you anything, he's a man seemingly obsessed with the end of times and saving people from getting left behind. And in his books, everything is a warning the end was near. Everything. The updated versions would for sure list Segway tours, poke salads, and dancing Gangnam style - as likely indications of the second coming. People get ready.

Standing over the tar pits, I remembered some of the things I had read in these books. I read about how Christians believed in Creationism, the idea that the Earth is only 6000 years old, different from the billions of years that scientists believe. I remember the book was so convincing with mathematical equations and proof from the Bible to counter any frivolous scientific argument. Like the three million bones from the Ice Age found right here in Los Angeles? Easy peasy lemon squeezy. The simple answer: dinosaurs and humans lived together at the same time. This rationale now rang with the same sensibility of a Greek dad advising to "Put some Windex on it." Standing mere feet from heavy, black tar said to be 10,000-40,000 years old, and amid my spiritual crisis, I realized that I avoided many scientific things because I was taught most scientists are atheists. And atheists are next to the devil. Making science the devil himself.

Right before I started at the Baptist university, one of my sisters wanted to attend a service at the local megachurch. My mom isn't a fan of crowds, but we all decided to go with her. It was so crowded, we arrived half an hour early, parked at the airport, and took the church shuttle over to the service. We walked past the church coffee shop, church restaurant, church bookstore, and several large classrooms to the large nursery to drop off my baby nephew. We got in the long line, and when it was our turn, a gruff lady with a mustache and a name tag labeled "Betty" helped us. My nephew was fussing when they took him back, but we thought he just needed a minute to adjust. We walked around to peek through a window to see if he calmed down. A nursery worker set him down with a toy, but he knew something was off. He looked around for his mom, and when he didn't see her, tears poured out. A younger worker walked up to him, smiled, and shook a colorful toy in front of him and walked away. He still cried. We went back and stood in line. When we made it up to the front, we told Betty we were going to take him into service with us.

Half smiling, she said boorishly, "You've gotta leave him some time, ma'am."

To which my sister replied, "Today is not that day."

Betty cupped her hands to her mouth and yelled back to the other workers, "I need number 17."

Another woman carried the baby, holding him sideways like a sack of potatoes, and passed him to us. He sighed in relief as he was placed back in my sister's arms.

Before we could step out of line, mustache lady went on, "Next."

This was me during the 2016 elections of Donald Trump and Hillary Clinton. Trump was supported largely by the evangelical Christian church and Hillary Clinton by a vast majority of everyone else. I was begging to know where God was in this mess, but all we got was mainstream pastors shaking colorful toys in attempts to appease the growing concern among many churchgoers. When it didn't work, they'd shout, "next" and move on to other church-attending recruits.

Like many others, I was shocked at the election but even more saddened by the evangelicals who called it a victory for Christianity. I felt sick from pastors in the front lines stood by and said nothing, or worse, promoted this political turmoil. After DACA was reversed, I saw Fox News Christians holding signs about gun rights that said, "Let's just call guns undocumented so they can stay." Cutting down the integrity and existence of a living-breathing human being, to the same as a tool used in war.

Dan Rather shared a poem by German anti-Nazi theologian Martin Niemöller, about the responsibility of his country to speak out in the surge of Nazism.

"First they came for the Socialists, and I did not speak out—
Because I was not a Socialist.
Then they came for the Trade Unionists,
and I did not speak out—
Because I was not a Trade Unionist.
Then they came for the Jews, and I did not speak out—
Because I was not a Jew.
Then they came for me—
and there was no one left to speak for me."

I believe the most significant stain on American Christianity will be the way we have handled the displaced. What did the Bible mean when it said that Jesus, "tore down the wall we used to keep each other at a distance." Where is the line drawn when evangelical leaders will say no more?

I was grieved at the church's response to this, meeting the marginalized with indifference and ignorance, and even more grieved by the notion my faith has been heavily influenced by these same people and ideals. I sank deeper into confusion and frustration with the church and saw an entirely new dimension of my Christian roots exposed.

21. Hello Northern California

I've heard plenty of church women say when their teens are stepping out of the house, they don't lecture them on how they should behave. They don't needle over the rules or review the curfew. They simply state the phrase, "Remember who you are." This is to signal the teen to all the home-training and Christian values their family upholds. I get the idea, but I've always found this a bit foolish, considering they are addressing teenagers, who typically exist solely within an identity crisis and have no idea who they are. They are navigating the opposite sex, discerning friendships, juggling school assignments, and attempting to answer the monumental question of what they will do after graduation. As a teen, I felt lost and a little unsure. The statement "remember who you are" causes me to pause every time. Maybe because I heard it first at church. Perhaps because I think about who I am with God. I had no idea. But I'm convinced the feeling of being unsure doesn't go away.

We had new orders to Humboldt Bay in Northern California, a place I never heard of despite living in the same state almost my entire life. On our last night living in Washington state, I reminisced about all the happenings of the previous two years. The ways I had been uprooted and stretched as a wife and mom. And how much I had gone through spiritually. It had been a rough going for God and me. I was ready for a fresh start — a new place. Reasonably I could arrive a little more together than when I came to Washington state. Hopefully, I will leave here, remembering more of who I am.

The movers arrived, and I wasn't mentally prepared. Yeah, I know it's part of the deal. That is, moving every two to four years comes with being a Coast Guard spouse. I knew our perfect townhouse wouldn't be our forever home, but I didn't anticipate getting so attached.

At nearly 2:30 am, I could hear my two-year-old start to whimper. I carefully walked into his room, shuffling my feet across the floor, dodging legos, and other small toys that covered the floor like confetti falling out of a birthday card. As hard as I try to pick it all up, there is always more confetti. I found myself staring at my firstborn. His delicate skin. Rosy cheeks. Thick eyelashes. His face was angelic. I took his chubby little boy hand and kissed his forehead, breathing him in and savoring it.

Glancing around the dim room, I felt the pulse of heartbreak. I didn't want to leave this house. It was the house where my baby crawled and stood and walked for the first time. It wasn't just the house, but all the transitions of the last two years. Since arriving here, we had celebrated Evan's first birthday and brought our second baby, Ethan, home from the hospital. I made new friends, lost a best friend, mended broken family relationships, and watched enough Mickey Mouse to be considered a negligent parent. I had to learn my way around. New freeways. New friends. New grocery stores. The grocery stores are the absolute worst. It should be a mandate that all grocery stores must be set up the same way. It would save me endless hours of doubling back to see if the sunflower seeds are in the chip aisle with the snacking peanuts or the baking aisle with the almonds. But it doesn't matter. All this will be gone tomorrow, and I will have to start over.

As I inched back into bed, my husband must have sensed my sadness because he pulled me in tight and kissed my head. I laid in the dimness, listening to the window fan and my dogs' snoring. I told myself again, to stay present because both skipping ahead and looking back is wasteful.

If you've never made a military move with two little kids, I wouldn't recommend it unless you're the kind of person who enjoys things such as kicking yourself in the face repeatedly. I spent three days giving directions to the movers and taking inventory of all our items I hoped would make it to the other side. I canceled utilities, our gym memberships, and changed our address with the USPS. I scheduled the carpet cleaners, washed all the laundry, and started a separate pile for the things we would keep in the car with us. I packed for the kids: diapers and extra pacifiers and The Blankie; dear God, do not forget that. I packed for the dogs. Snacks for the family. Bottles for the baby. Pack-N-Plays and strollers for both boys. All of these things plus family photos, laptops, and anything else the movers aren't taking. Then Jeff and I killed an hour trying to configure everything in the cars while leaving room for the actual humans and dogs. After we returned keys to the landlord and said goodbye to our neighbors, we started our drive. It was a total of five minutes before Evan was hungry, and Ethan needed a clean diaper. We stopped roughly 2,378 times to fix car seats, dole out feedings, take bathroom breaks, and refuel.

We planned to drive until we got tired and then find a hotel on the route. About midpoint, we decided to start looking for a place to sleep. I called a few hotels and found them all fully booked for the night. We called a few more. No vacancy.

I somewhat panicked after one hotel guy laughed at me, "Lady, it's summer on the Oregon coast. You're not going to find a room."

157

Between Jeff and I, we phoned no fewer than fifty hotels - no exaggeration. Finally, one place had a room available. We had to drive about an hour inland, but at least it was a room.

Grumpy and tired, we pulled into the "luxury hotel" we could see was unquestionably a low-star motel and likely the kind we could rent by the hour. Jeff went into the office, and I waited in the car with the boys. I noticed a scantily dressed woman wandering in and out of rooms. Her name was likely whatever I wanted it to be. There were three large, hairy men smoking on the steps. One man had a tear-drop tattoo, or maybe it was a drooping mole. I looked harder — definitely a tear-drop. And when I observed the cops drive up and yell out to one of them, "Hey Smiley, come here," I was texting Jeff in the office. *No way I'm staying here. They're on a first-name basis with the cops!* Assuming, of course, Smiley was his real name.

Jeff walked out to me in the car, and I rolled the window down. He said he agreed, but there wasn't anywhere else open.

He sighed. "I'll just glance in the room and see what it's like. Wait here."

But when he went to unlock the door, it was already cracked. The TV was on, and sounds were coming from the bathroom. We hightailed it out but with nowhere to go. Phoning more hotels only landed us further and further inland until we found one in Portland, Oregon - a few hours off our driving route. But at least it was ours. It was a Marriott hotel, of course. I sent a silent blessing to Mr. Marriott, and we checked in. I was exhausted and ready to pass out, but not before hauling our things from the car into the hotel and taking the dogs out to potty. I got the boys into their nighties and put them to bed. Of course, they didn't want to sleep because they had napped the whole car ride. Plus, nothing is more fun than playing with the phone and mini-fridge. Nobody really slept.

In the morning, we dragged everything back to the cars and hit the road. At nearly midnight, we arrived at Humboldt Bay in

Northern California, but before we could go to our new house, we had to stop by the Coast Guard station to pick up the keys our landlord left for us. Finally, we arrived at the house I had only seen photos of but would be living in for the next three years. Streetlights highlighted the darkness. I could make out the shape of the green two-story house, and it seemed okay enough. The house had siding, not stucco, like the homes where I grew up, and there was an extended two-car garage. Jeff unlocked the doors, and a restless Evan ran circles around the interior of the home.

As Jeff lugged our suitcases in the house, I peeked around. I instantly like the house. A lot bigger than our townhouse in Washington, with four generous sized rooms, a dining room, living room, and formal room. Older Berber carpet, which is perfect. I wouldn't have to agonize over each little kid spill. And from what I could make out, the backyard was enormous. I got Evan in his pajamas and changed Ethan's diaper. When I went to the sink to wash my hands, there was no water. No showers, no sink water, no toilet flushing after midnight. We called and paid $200 for the water company to turn on the water. Perfect.

Safe in our new house, Jeff blew up the air mattress, and I put the kids to bed. Depleted from the motel saga and the lengthy drive, I collapsed into bed and was soothed by a soft whistling sound until I realized our air mattress had a hole. The next day I woke to a deflated air mattress and my back in knots. We set up the rest of the utilities and scheduled the cable guy. We went to Kmart, the only store in town, and purchased new curtain rods and hand towels and updated the dog's tags with our new address. After five days of living in an empty house, and sleeping on an empty air mattress, the moving truck arrived. As they parked the semitrailer, they ran over the neighbor's basketball court, a great way to meet our neighbors. Thankfully it didn't break. They strong-armed the truck open, brandishing all our household items, and as they carried our things into the house, I took inventory and wrangled my toddler from getting crushed by the stacked boxes. Nine hours later, we signed a mass of paperwork, and the movers departed.

I attempted to unpack but had to stop every few minutes. I stopped to feed whichever child was hungry or crying. I stopped for attempted naps. I stopped at a grocery store for all new food. I stopped for tantrums and spills and to put on another Disney show.

As I was unpacking the linen cabinet, I heard nothing. The house was oddly peaceful. I should have gone to look for Evan, but I gave myself a moment to appreciate it. I had prepared the best I could for the move, and it had left me drained, but now the real work commences. Making this house a home. I imagined what memories this house might hold in a few years. I already missed my old house and the quaint town of Poulsbo, but I knew the worst habit I could start was comparing my past with my present. I told myself again, to stay present because skipping ahead and looking back are wasteful. In the times of getting lost, finding my way around town, or not having local friends, I will stop and let myself miss our last place. But then, as all military spouses must, I will resolve to live in the present, learn new freeways and make new friends. And alas, to make my way around a new grocery store.

22. Downsizing Small Group

My hometown friends ask me how I do it, all this moving around and such. The truth is, I love it. Yeah, it's hard, but at this point in my life, I couldn't envision living in one area permanently. There's something mystical about being submerged in a new city, discovering the history and culture and economy. Meeting the people and learning what makes it unique. The world is one colossal, kaleidoscope, made of one container, but with every twist, the view is entirely diverse.

Before we moved to Humboldt, Jeff came for a week of training and was able to see the area. He called me from the hotel the first night. I was at home. I had just laid Evan down and was nursing the baby.

"Tell me everything," I instructed.

He hesitated, "Well, uh, it's different."

The hesitation should have been the big clue, but I didn't read it. I shifted the baby to the opposite boob.

"Different how?" I pressed him.

He did his best to describe it. "Okay, It's like if you took the chillaxness of San Diego, the weather of Seattle, and time-warped back to the 70s - you'd have this place."

Cool, I thought. I relished living in San Diego and near Seattle, so Humboldt was going to be amazing. I had unknowingly neglected the part about being time-warped to the 1970s. Making our way to Humboldt, I saw the jaw-dropping coastlines and trees wider than Suburbans, but once you hit the little town we would be living in, I was majorly disappointed. I might have been more impressed by eating rice cakes and watching CSPAN. There was a Kmart and also a Denny's and a disproportionate number of gardening shops, but I didn't understand why. There were very few trees on the main street. Most, I assume, were eliminated in the logging days. I was expecting lines of redwood trees and quaint cabin restaurants that overlooked the water.

Even though many people think it's remarkably beautiful here, I thought it was so ugly. I felt guilty and scolded myself because I can acutely recall judging something my girlfriend, Lora Beth, had said a few years earlier when we both had just moved to Washington state. She came from Juneau, Alaska, and I came from D.C. While I couldn't get over how breathtaking Washington was, she wasn't impressed. She commented on how it was just mediocre compared to Alaska, and I thought she was crazy. Perspective is everything.

I gave myself a tiny little pep-talk. *Don't jump to conclusions. You haven't seen everything. We are going to settle in, make friends, and it's going to be great!* A crystal ball would have revealed that Humboldt would be our most arduous move yet. I was tired-as-a-mother. And my boys, the sweetest things on planet Earth, were adapting to the move in their own challenging ways. I looked for things to do while Jeff was at work, but there weren't many places I felt comfortable going on my own. The idea that shocked me the most about this area was the high crime rate. We tried to walk to the local Hammond trail, a path by the water, but there were always groups of men hiding in the bushes doing who knows what. We visited the neighborhood park twice. Both times, nobody else was there besides the drunk homeless group assembled under the pergola, growing louder with every swig, only stopping to walk across the mobile tightrope they had tied between the benches.

Outside the main strip of McKinleyville, there was charm. More like I had anticipated the Redwoods would be, it just took me a while to find it. Overall I was underwhelmed. I heard Humboldt is part of what they call the Emerald Triangle, three counties in Northern California that grow about 70% of America's marijuana, which could explain the gardening shops and unyielding waves of skunk smell within an objective twenty-mile radius. The town might seriously benefit from partnering with Summer's Eve. For the first three months, I woke nearly every night to skunk smell coming into the second-story window of my bedroom. The potency made my eyes water. But even more than Mary Jane, I was taken off guard with the crime from heroin and methamphetamine. The Redwoods was supposed to be a family-friendly camping area, not have the same crime rates of major cities.

Once, on the way home from work, one of the Coast Guard guys was yanked from his car and assaulted while driving on the 101 highway. I didn't feel safe and didn't know anyone, so I stayed home. I wanted to get away and visit my parents, but even though we lived in the same state, it was a 13-hour drive. On the awful days, I contemplated making the trip. My sister asked if we lived close to San Francisco because Southern Californians, like me, considered San Francisco to be "Northern California."

Yes," I said bitterly. "Like, a stone's throw, if you're able to throw a stone the distance of a five-hour drive, up and down steep mountains, with nearly no cell phone reception and routine closures from mud-slides."

A guaranteed excellent drive with cranky toddlers. Flying out was harder on the pocketbook. A direct flight out of Humboldt quickly added $400 to a standard ticket price for a likely delayed flight due to blanket fog. We stayed home. My optimism was deserting me.

Since our leaving options were limited, we tried to find our place. We went church shopping again and came across a church that assembled in the local town center, in a gymnasium. There were folding chairs arranged in rows and a riser stage with black curtains in the front. Unlike D.C., they didn't have perfect systems in place, professional lighting, or a concert-like feel. It was a modest non-denominal small church with contemporary worship music and seemed as sound as any other church we would find elsewhere. It was very similar to all the other small-town churches we tried. Friendly and unpolished.

Once again, we looked to join a small group. There was only one, and it wasn't kid-friendly. I consorted with the gym childcare workers and hired one to watch Evan while we tried the group. When the sitter arrived, I read her way too many instructions from my two pages of typed babysitter notes. We took Ethan with us and drove to the small group held in the house of a church member. I disliked going from day one. But, I never really gave it a fair shot. The people were friendly, but I had no energy and a fussy four-month-old. Motherhood and moving left me spent, and I didn't feel like myself. I stood in the corner of the living room endlessly bouncing Ethan, while striving to make awkward conversations with people I was too drained to get to know. I also resented paying $40 for the babysitter to spend our time further exhausting myself, instead of doing something fun, like a date. I was depressed. And that made it all worse. I didn't want to feel cynical and sad, but I didn't know how to stop it.

The group picked the book *Crazy Love* by Francis Chan, and I thought, *Good Lord, here we go again*. It was almost amusing the way these books kept coming back to me. The first night, we watched a video clip that corresponded to the book, and seeing Francis Chan

164

speak, gave me a new perspective on his writing voice. He didn't sound as jackassy in the video as I had interpreted the book earlier. While I still didn't agree with everything in the book, I didn't spite him as much. Of course, I didn't tell the group this. I previously decided I wasn't going to share any grievances with the church because I had just met everyone. And, as it turned out, we went only three times before quitting.

My depression deepened. I knew I had to make a choice. To be a depressed hermit for the next three years or find something good about living here. I grabbed my purse and my giant bottle of pepper spray and took the boys on a walk through the ugly town. I forced myself to find a dozen things I liked about it. I repeated this almost daily. On the days I saw nothing good, I would look up to the sky and thank God for the sun and clouds and air. I joined a gym with childcare a few miles over in the town of Arcata, and I joined the local MOPS group. The days were slowly getting better. Sometimes I was hard-pressed to find the good, but if I worked for it, I invariably found something.

We decided to get away and take our first family-of-four vacation. Five if you count our pup. All of us, German Shepherd included, squished into my Jeep Rubicon, and we started the four-hour drive to Lake Shasta. It was a long ride, and there was crying. The boys cried too. Evan said, "It's really far. We should take an airplane."

And I agreed. He asked for a snack every five minutes, and I starved him out of fear he would throw up like he always does on a winding road. I didn't feel bad because we arrived at the cabin in a clean car.

The boys were beyond enthusiastic about the lake cabin. They ran around with huge, animated grins as they forced open every drawer and cupboard. Thankfully, it was mostly child-proof. It was nearing bedtime, but we all sat on the deck outside at the big wooden table. Jeff and Evan on one side of the table. Ethan and I sat on the opposite side. We ate Chipotle while overlooking the lake and then wandered to the snack shop for ice cream. Evan attempted to ride his tiny skateboard, and Ethan giggled. After bedtime prayers and snuggles, Jeff and I sat outside in the quiet and watched the sunset over the lake. This moment, right here, merited the long car ride and the crying. The twilight and chilly night air paired with the beautiful silence was perfect.

The next day we rented a boat, and Evan had his first boat driving lesson from our Coastie. Ethan cried the first hour and then fell asleep in my arms. I kissed his chubby pink cheeks, and I briefly forgot about the crying. Briefly. Until he woke.

Back at the cabin, Jeff fired up the grill to cook our steaks and veggies skewers. Two minutes in, we noticed way too much smoke emitting from the BBQ.

"Jeff, is it supposed to look like that?"

My concern was growing as a thick black cloud formed over our cabin. We opened it, and everything was on fire. Jeff hurriedly switched off the propane, but the fire only got more extreme. The cabin was too close, and we feared the fire spreading. I hastily dialed the office and said we needed a fire extinguisher ASAP. By the time the fire was out, our dinner was ruined. We discovered the grill hadn't been maintained properly, and it caused the fire. Jeff picked up takeout, and we spent the evening on the deck with wine and sunset.

The next morning, the boys woke way too early. We said we wouldn't turn on the television, but on day three, we succumbed to the temptation of Paw Patrol. Later that day, we all bundled up to tour the caverns, a national landmark at Lake Shasta. It was nearly 100 outside, but the locals warned it would be very chilly. The website, which I didn't read until after, says, "There is an extensive walking component of the tour, and it is not recommended for people suffering from heart conditions, knee or back issues, or other medical conditions." They're missing, "or moms that plan on carrying a fidgety one-year-old for the tour." As there were over 600 stairs, I had to trek while holding Ethan. He pushed away from me and cried. Uphill. Both ways. Okay, maybe not, but at this moment, I felt empathy for Sacagawea climbing the Rockies with a baby. I huffed up the stairs carrying the whiny child, and I made comments to Jeff that I'm pretty sure require some sort of forgiveness. Also, I forgot my shoes and had to wear Jeff's way-too-big running shoes. And I could see people whispering and pointing at my circus feet. Midpoint on the tour, I didn't care anymore about the caverns or all the beauty. It might as well be a pile of dirt. I just wanted to be done and get back to my lake cabin and lounge on the deck. And we did.

The view allowed me to overlook my Lewis and Clark Expedition, and we ordered a pizza. No cooking or cleaning required. I sat on the deck and wondered about the vacations we took when I was little. Was it this much work for my parents too? Surely, my brother and I were the exceptions, and my parents were able to relax and unwind. I mean, it was totally a vacation for my parents too. Right?

All good things must come to an end. We packed the car and started the journey back home. Evan asked for snacks, and I caved. He threw up, and Ethan cried. At home, I had to unpack. And I had laundry, but thankfully only a little because I made them wear the same thing every day. Strategies.

23. Downsizing Hell

A few months after we had arrived in Humboldt, I talked to the local church about hosting the IF:Gathering, the same conference I attended in Washington for the last two years. Our church leaders were excited about it, and we set up to host about forty women. Looking back at my life, I was crazy to take on a project like this. Evan was almost three, and Ethan was only six months. But something in my little event-planning-heart wanted this.

When the conference arrived, I wasn't able to listen to most of the speakers because I was in event coordinating mode — running around, keeping things moving along and on schedule. I caught a few moments here and there. All the women were enjoying themselves and seemed very interested in the topics and speakers. The women nodded in agreement when speaker Eugene Cho challenged the notion that the grass is greener on the other side with the prompt we should, "Water the grass we are standing on. Water our marriage, our friendships, our families, our calling. Water right where we are."

The older women cried Amen, and the younger ones scribbled notes in their journals. There was worship and prayer and scripture reading. It was all so anointed. There was story sharing, tears shed, and deep connections made over meals. It felt beautiful and captivating. I believe connecting with other women is one of the most sacred gifts.

Nearing the end of the conference, I sat down in time to hear a short clip of the last speaker, David Platt, telling a story in which the situation leads him to say to a woman point-blank, she was going to hell since she didn't believe in Jesus. The message conveyed that it's unloving for us not to share the truth of Jesus, even when it's offensive. People need to hear it, and we should not be afraid to share the gospel. Basically, we aren't doing anyone favors by tiptoeing around their feelings. I felt my shoulders tighten and an immediate taste of embarrassment at his attitude. *Well, this is pretty divisive*, I thought. But even though I didn't think the talk fit the heart of the conference, the message of going to hell was in alignment with most Christian views I had grown up with. Here, it seemed more aggressive and a bit out of place for the rest of the conference. I guess I couldn't say because I hadn't seen many of the speakers before him. And just like that, it was over.

I thanked everyone for coming, and someone closed us in prayer. As the ladies shuffled out, one of the women stayed behind. She stood in the kitchen, distraught with tears streaming down her face, she said, for all her non-believing friends who are going to hell. She said she needed to stop messing around and unapologetically tell them the truth so that they can be saved. I didn't know what to say to her, but luckily, a more seasoned woman was already consoling her.

Afterward, in the *Facebook* group for leaders of the local groups, someone expressed concern about the approach of telling people they are going to hell. A few agreed. A few didn't. But everyone had an opinion. One woman shared that during this portion of the conference, a few unbelieving women up and walked out, some of them crying. Another said she regretted sharing the conference on social media because of how this was approached, and she hoped her unbelieving friends didn't watch the link she posted. Some agreed with the message but not the delivery. Some didn't agree with the speaker's theology. Some said American Christians are so complacent. Some said they were happy the message wasn't watered down, and we can't stop sharing because we might offend people. Some said it was good if they were offended because it planted seeds, and we shouldn't be afraid of sharing. Some said we would answer to God for all the people we don't share the gospel with. Some said it's okay if we ruffle feathers. Because Jesus did. One person even said that the gospel is offensive, and our hearts "must" be offended in some way. Wait. *What?*

Didn't Jesus ruffle the feathers of church leaders and the religious people of his time? The ones who were put off by his inclusion? The ones who were dismayed with Jesus' lack of reverence for their theology and rules? I wondered how we can all look at the same Christ and see the complete opposite message. But what do I know? Pretty much nothing. And if I remember correctly, the woman from the speaker's story - the one he told outright was going to hell - well, she accepted Jesus that summer - so it worked out perfectly. But what about for the ones it doesn't work out?

We like to believe all this blunt truth-telling and gospel sharing is helping. We call it planting seeds, but do we have proof of this seed planting? Is there a statistic that shows for everyone we tell is going to hell, the percentage of people who will convert? I wonder if I asked my Christian friends, what led them to God, how many of them would list their main reason being to avoid hell? Is it rooted in the love of God, or is it an insurance policy?

It bothered me that the conference ended on such a stark note, but I got fantastic feedback from the women who had attended our local event. I knew the two years I had watched the conferences in its entirety were wonderful. As I wrapped up the event, I considered if Christianity was changing, or was it me? I went home to my exhausted husband and my babies but continued to wonder about the idea of saving people from hell.

Not long after the conference, I came across a new idea about hell. That hell was less a place for after death, but a state of mind in which we are absent from God or are rejecting the love of God. Hell was the dark parts of life. To choose Christ over hell was choosing the morally right and loving, over fear, shame, and sadness. Choosing love puts us in connection with God. While selecting fear puts us in hell.

This idea was fascinating to me, considering I grew up in the evangelical church, and a stark visual was drawn about hell. I was taught that hell is a place where people who rejected Christ would literally be tortured and burn forever. There would be weeping and gnashing of teeth and eternal damnation. Hell was a central part of the evangelical message because it was where everyone who wasn't *saved* was going. You cannot go to heaven if you haven't accepted Christ as your Lord and Savior, likely by the Sinner's Prayer. Both the people who choose not to believe it and the ones who died before they could hear the good message are going to hell, which is why there was so much pressure placed on evangelizing. I've been to a handful of churches that proudly tout the number of people saved in their service, using it as polling analytics with the goal of having more visitors, a low bounce rate, and ultimately people to buy in and become believers.

Stepping out of my bubble, I was surprised to learn how many other Christian denominations didn't believe this same idea of hell and rapture. I heard the person who had overseen the writing of the Nicene Creed, a widely used statement of beliefs for Catholics, didn't believe in this idea of hell either. The point is that the issues are nuanced and not black and white like I was taught. Even the Baptist minister, Martin Luther King Jr., didn't believe in the same idea of hell.

Martin Luther King Jr. wrote:

"We must not take this story as a theology of the afterlife. It is not a Baedeker's guide to the next world. Its symbols are symbols and not literal fact. Jesus accepted the hereafter as a reality but never sought to describe it. There is always the danger that we will transform mythology into theology. We must remember that there is always a penumbra of mystery which hovers around every meaningful assertion about God and the afterlife. He who seeks to describe the furniture of heaven and the temperature of hell is taking the mystery out of religion and incarcerating it in the walls of an illogical logic. Jesus had no such intentions. He was merely telling a parable to get over a basic truth about this life. He who takes this parable as a description of the history and geography of the afterlife is transplanting it violently from its native soil to a barren literalism where it cannot live."

A few weeks after the conference, I sat in the somewhat conservative church we were attending. A guest pastor was speaking who mentioned he didn't think hell was an actual place either. *I knew it!*

I read that at the time Jesus walked the Earth, there wasn't a word for hell, and there wasn't a word for another 700 years. The people who translated the Bible took several other words used in Biblical stories and turned them into the word hell. One of these words is Gehenna, an actual physical place in Jerusalem, used as the town dump. The bodies of the unclaimed were thrown here and burned alongside the trash. I learned that depending on your church denomination, views on hell were all over the map, not just the one way I had learned. Many Biblical scholars, who devote their entire lives to studying the Bible, argue the meaning of hell. And if they can't agree, why does the church push teaching this as an absolute?

Recently a friend sent me this message:

"I am a strong advocate of religious tolerance. I personally believe every religion contains aspects of truth. So I don't think there's just one "right" way. Compassion, empathy, peace, patience, understanding- these are ideals I think we all rightly strive for.

I had a conversation with someone dear to me that made it crystal clear she is certain any person who does not follow the path of Jesus and accept the resurrection as absolute historical truth is going to hell. No exceptions. She even said that, yes, all Buddhists and the Dalai Lama himself are going to hell. (I have great reverence for Eastern traditions). This person clearly expressed one can never be "good enough" to get into heaven without having "accepted" Jesus. This person also (without being rude about it) admitted that, yes, my current beliefs would place me in hell (though she doesn't want to see that happen to me and thinks Jesus will save me). The person claimed to make no personal judgment of me but knew what God's judgment would be. I know this is not atypical of Christian fundamentalists, but it was still strange to hear in a personal, one-on-one conversation. I've known the role and perspective of religion in this person's life and had been fairly closed-mouthed about some of my beliefs until directly asked. I see religious texts (Bible included) as holding universal truths about the human condition. I personally don't think it matters if the resurrection really happened or not. But, the point of this isn't to get into all the ins and outs of my mashed up Western and Eastern beliefs.

I didn't want to argue against my friend's beliefs. I wouldn't want to in any way strip away from her what is such a powerful and important aspect of her life and worldview. But I can't help but be bothered by her perspective, and now I find myself wondering if my dismay in and of itself is a failure to uphold my own beliefs about religious tolerance. But it bothers me when someone thinks their way is the only way.

Is it fair to say everyone can have their own beliefs, ideas and opinions as long as they don't project them onto others? Is that part of religious tolerance? My head is so spun."

Likely, this conversation would have been deemed "seed-planting" by her friend. But it's rather one that pushes people further away from Christianity. I know some might be thinking, well, you never know what God will do with these kinds of conversations. But I'd argue that these aren't conversations. This is Christians talking at people, not with them, based on absolutes that come with their faith. A real discussion would be to consider and learn from each other. Not come to the table with all the answers. And while it's most likely from a loving place, this wanting to share Jesus with everyone and get people saved, it comes across as condescending and exclusive rather than an intense theological conversation about our beliefs of God and Life and Love.

As I worked through all this faith stuff, deciding what to keep and toss, being asked such a direct question about hell from my beautiful friend left me trying to piece together some of my thoughts. I told her that this is the kind of thing I grew up learning, but I don't see it as truth. I find it divisive. It creates an *us* and a *them*. People who are "saving" and those who need to be "saved." At its worst, it can create a savior complex for the Christians, not for God. It creates a team to join. Many will find a sense of belonging within the team. A way to help them define their identity because, as humans, we innately want to know who we are. Having someone tell us the answer makes it uncomplicated. Collectivity, we have a massive identity crisis. Religion can fill that void. So can a street gang. How and why some Christians make such statements, like, the Dalai Lama is going to hell, is beyond me. I do believe there is some truth in every religion, and many religions overlap. Christianity and Islam might have the most in common. The Sinner's Prayer, or ideas of a "personal relationship" with God, isn't in the Bible, not that this can't exist, but they are interpretations of what people think the Bible says.

Gradually, I've quit the evangelical version of hell. I don't think hell is a place where non-believers are sent after we die. I think if Jesus only mentions hell a handful of times, and hell wasn't even a word, and it was translated during a time when people thought God deliberately used rain and storms and fire to punish and judge, then it seems likely this has been grossly misinterpreted. In Jesus's time, the current religion wasn't loving. Jesus's message was of love and radical acceptance, and it was shocking to people. Sometimes I think we forget this. I see some churches ruled by dogma and theology. We all want certainty. We believe the "right" way, but certainty is the opposite of faith. Coming to the table with certainty robs us of plentiful conversations about history and God.

Years ago, I thought fundamentalists were the people wearing prairie dresses and holding up hateful signs outside abortions clinics, but now I see the fundamentalism in most of the underlying evangelical message. And it breaks my heart. However, my friend brings up a good point about having religious tolerance. As I move through my spiritual crisis, I've lost my patience too many times. I've been frustrated that people think the message of God *must* offend people. I get pissed off when people are okay with, and proud of, a message hurting people, while painting it as telling the truth in love or seed planting or social martyrdom for the sharing of Christ. All of this has left me undone.

However, in the process of shifting my views, have I become the exact mirror of the things I dislike most in the church? Have I grown a tolerance for the other religions but lost it for the one I used to love? Have I been willing to offend, because it's my truth? Where is my tolerance? Where is my love? I don't know anything other than sometimes I'm terrible at all this. Maybe religious tolerance is holding space for people. If I can give myself space to just be, or evolve, then I have to make room for them just to be or evolve when and if they need to. And to keep showing up. Not pushing my differences aside or hiding, but to hear and still love.

24. Downsizing the House

As much as I wanted, I couldn't hold space for anyone, because I was out of space. Mentally and physically. I realized this one evening as I carried the boy's toys upstairs, along with a basket of laundry and some other little random stuff. I stopped and looked around. Things never seem to stay put away, and all I did was walk my house collecting items that needed a home — all day long.

There were dishes, laundry, grocery shopping, menu planning, changing sheets, changing diapers, paying bills, and trying to manage it all. And somewhere in all of this, I was supposed to find my purpose? Love my children with the patience of Mother Teresa. Have meaningful sex with my husband every day. Get my pre-baby body back. Balance a budget. Meditate and pray and be spiritual. And don't forget to make self-care a priority. Lord, help me.

That night, just after 1:00 am, I rubbed my eyes and sighed as I attempted to lay my crying baby boy down for the third time. I crawled back into bed and dared to place my head on my pillow, hoping I wouldn't have to get up again, but I knew I'd be up for another hour thinking about the things I thought of every night. It was always the same tape playing over and over. My church issues, the list of things I need to fix and clean, the stuff I hadn't done, relationships that need mending, how I lost my patience with the boys too many times that day, and how in the world was I ever going to pay off my student loans. My anxiety was coming on. Maybe I was also sleep-deprived, not uncommon for motherhood. Perhaps I'd gone crazy. Likely, both.

I listened to the window fan and my dog's collar rustling in the dark, and I thought about how I got there — married for about five years with two kids at foot and a decent-sized home with a two-car garage. The American dream at its best. Then why was I still unsettled, exhausted, and overwhelmed? This wasn't what I signed up for. I don't remember everyone saying, get married, and have kids, so you can be exhausted and clean all day. Did I shave my legs for this?

I was trying to be a June Cleaver. Clean house, well-behaved kids, dinner on time, and forever wearing dresses and pearls. However, I'm not June. I'm more of a Lucy Ricardo. I make more mischief and messes than I clean, and I burn dinner regularly. I thought about how women are taught and measured by our ability to create a home and to make it inviting. Decorate with pretty stuff. Have crafty things at hand so our kids will be creative. Keep it all organized. The message society gives us about marriage and motherhood and keeping a home: Make it perfect. Look amazing. Pretend it happens seamlessly.

If this is true, and women are to create the home environment, who decides the *right* way it should look? These rules, the ones I was taught, it's programming. So the story goes, a newly married wife is cooking a pot roast dinner for her new husband. She pulls out a roast, cuts off both ends, and cooks it.

Her husband, curious, asks her, "Why are you cutting the ends of the roast? It's the best part!"

She replies, "That's the way my mom did it." The next week while at tea with her mom, the young wife asks why she cut the ends of the roast.

Her mother replied, "Hmh, I'm not sure. That's the way my mom cooked it."

Both of the women were now wondering, and the next Sunday at Grandma's house as they were cooking dinner asked, "Grandma, why do you cut the roast ends off?"

The grandmother replied, "Because my pan is too small."

Was I unknowingly chopping off the best parts of life because I had yet to question why? During 99% of my day-in-day-out activities, I never wonder why or if they are necessary, or holding me back or hurting my ability to live free because it's how I've seen it done. And that's where I lost it. The combination of past generation's teachings, and the things I learned from my education, media, and society, means that most of what I do, I've not consciously chosen. And worse, I've let unconscious decisions define my roles, my success in marriage, motherhood, careers, and womanhood. I am a Stepford wife. And for the record, this is not about passing the blame on to people or society because I believe most people, myself included, can be innocent, unconscious to our detriment. I was ready to wake up, to stop being numb, and to learn why.

The house, the stuff, and the pressure, it was all just too much. The big house we eagerly moved into was meant for us to enjoy, but all my time was spent moving from one room to the next, trying to keep up and failing miserably. By the time I would sit down with my husband and boys, I was exhausted. I hit my breaking point. A pivot became necessary for the survival of my soul. I knew there had to be a better way. I could have gotten down on my knees and prayed, but I needed to make a different kind of prayer. The type of prayer that requires actual sweat and would leave me physically tired and sore and recklessly running towards a better life.

A few months before this, I wrote a goal to create a life I didn't need a vacation from. One of my best friends told me it sounded too cliché. Too Pinteresty. But I knew we needed a change and started evaluating the things I loved; spending time with my hubby, little adventures with the kids, running my business, and writing. Everything else needed an overhaul. I didn't know how this would look until I was packing for a trip. Jeff had to work in San Francisco, and the boys and I decided to tag along. It took me an entire day to pack for just two nights away.

Later that weekend, all four of us were sitting on the king-sized bed in the hotel when I pitched my idea to Jeff.

"What if we sold all our stuff and moved into an RV full time?" I was obsessed with tiny homes, and an RV had the added benefit of easy mobility. Ohh, the places we could go with no need for packing and unpacking, less cleanup, and sleeping in my own bed every night while traveling.

He thought I had officially gone insane. "You want to get rid of all our stuff?"

"Uh-huh," I said wistfully.

"And live in a space smaller than this hotel room?" There was concern in his voice.

"Yep." My grin was too wide, but I couldn't help it. I *knew* this was a great idea.

Jeff stared at me, blankly.

We talked about it a little more that night and searched Google. When we started researching, we found full-time RV living is actually a thing. There's an entire community of full-time families. Minutes later, I was sold and already planning what I would do with all the time I'd have if I weren't always trying to pick up toys and find places to put things away. A few days later, Jeff said yes, and we started making plans. I wondered what it would be like to wake up and be on the road in an hour. To not have to worry about bringing food because our kitchen was with us. To live on permanent vacation, while still doing everyday life. I pictured weekends on the Oregon coast, Klamath, Shasta, and many drives along the California coast.

We decided to take a chance because sometimes it's not enough to make little changes. Sometimes you need to go big or go home and make a massive change. To become obsessed with a new way of living that allows freedom and adventure. We only had 18 months left in Humboldt. I reasoned that I could do anything for 18 months, right? If we hated it, we could move back to a house, but at least we tried it, right?

25. Downsizing My Spiritual Fantasy Self

"Edit your life frequently and ruthlessly.
It's your masterpiece, after all."
~ Nathan W. Morris

Our evenings were spent hunting for just the right RV. By day, I was taking care of the boys and planning another IF:Gathering women's conference. When the weekend arrived, I was a little hesitant after last year's warnings on hell, but during the announcements, I started by telling the group that perhaps not everything we hear is for us, and that's okay, but it was my hope they would go with what they needed. Some call this notion of not accepting everything as being a "Cafeteria Christian" - a slight on the lack of dedication to the truth by going through the food line and only taking what we wanted. Still, it was advice I was regularly using with the church, and it was the only thing keeping my church relationship alive.

We had about 60 women attend, and I caught bits and pieces of the conference. I loved the parts I saw, especially the social justice and racial reconciliation segment. The group loved Jill Briscoe and her message, "Go where you are sent, and you stay where you're put, and you give what you've got." There was no hell-talk, and after two days, the conference ended. I breathed a huge sigh of relief and then ran home to start maybe my biggest project yet. Downsizing my life to 375 square feet.

We searched for months until we found the perfect RV for our family. At the top of my wish list were a bathtub, king-size bed, and a washer and dryer. We landed on a 44' Heartland RoadWarrior toy hauler. It had a master room and a garage conversion for the boys, a second bathroom, and most importantly, it hit all three items on my wish list. From all the RVs we looked at, this kitchen was the largest with a U-shaped countertop. The boy's room had two dropdown queen beds, but my dad built them toddler-size bunk beds. But the best part, the thing that made this RV perfect for us, was the enclosed side patio, which acted as a large playpen for the boys. I was beside myself. Not so much for all the trips we would take, yes, they would be amazing, but selfishly, I was excited not to have so much stuff around. What would I be doing all day if I wasn't always picking up toys?

But first, now that we had this tiny home, we had to downsize, which meant getting rid of a lot of things and moving from a big four-bedroom house to a tiny 375 square foot RV. We made dozens of trips to the local mission to drop off donations. We sold a few things and gave a bunch away. It took several very long days because downsizing is a full-time job.

We didn't want to keep much, but there was always a chance the military could send us somewhere we couldn't use the RV. We talked about getting rid of everything and buying things later if we needed them, but after calculating the cost of repurchasing mattresses, larger furniture, and a washer and dryer, it was cheaper to get a small storage unit for the year we would live in the RV. We kept the absolute bare minimum.

Letting go can be painful. When I was trying to declutter in preparation for moving, there were certain things I struggled to let go of. For example, we had an entire closet full of craft supplies for the boys: crayons, markers, paint, brushes, construction paper, and an endless stack of coloring books. My mom always had crafts projects for us when I was little, and I wanted my boys to embrace their creativity and love art. Therefore, it was my job as their mom to facilitate this, and the items stuffed in this closet was the proof I was doing my job. But now I had to decide what and how much to get rid of. I could only fit maybe ten percent of our stuff in the RV. I sat for hours trying to par down, but I couldn't. I felt that getting rid of these things would squash my boy's creativity, and I would fall short of my expectations as their mom.

Minimalist, Francine Jay, talks about the idea of her fantasy-self and the clutter we keep for her.

"All too often, we hold on to stuff because it represents who we think we should be, rather than who we are. Sometimes our fantasy selves are meant to impress others; sometimes they're relics of our past; sometimes they're fantasies about our future."

She goes on to ask: is your fantasy self a culinary diva who keeps endless kitchen gadgets, but you prefer takeout? Do you have a ton of fitness equipment but prefer to go hiking? Is your fantasy self a crafty person, but you never actually make anything? The stuff we keep for our fantasy self is a reminder of our shortcomings, and worse, it's stealing resources and space from the person we could become if we accepted our truths.

For the longest time, I kept a ton of kid's craft stuff because I believed it would help me be a better mom. But the truth is it was preventing me from being a better mom, because the cupboard was always overflowing, causing stress and annoyance whenever I thought about doing crafts with the boys.

The biggest struggle in letting go of an item is when I believe it says something about who I am or who I want to be. A thing I've unknowingly used to represent my ego and is tied up in my sense of importance. I try to tell myself stuff is just stuff. It shouldn't say anything about me unless I want it to. Ohh, but I do. I want my things to tell the world that I'm fashionable and smart, and I have it all together. I want people to think my kids are perfect angels, and my marriage is cloaked in twenty-four-seven romance and that I'm pretty much nailing all of life. More than telling the world, I want to believe it for myself. So, I keep the stuff, and I allow it to take the place of my ego, my identity, and my need for self-aggrandizement. This works as well as autocorrect on my phone.

Besides ego, one of the main reasons people fear letting go is scarcity. I keep things for my friend, Justin Case. Maybe you've met him? He offered his help as we took steps to make this massive change for our family. I had much to part with, and every time I'd try to let something go, Justin Case would butt-in. I found myself trying to purge, but thinking I should keep things *just in case*, get it? I know, corny dad joke. Seriously, though, I was upset by the amount of money I'd spent on things I was not using and thought maybe there's still a chance for them: a $50 breakfast-in-bed tray, a jacket a size too small but in a beautiful color, or impulse crafting items I needed. Nobody has brought me breakfast in bed on that beautiful tray. Ever. My first thought is, "Why did I buy this?" Followed by, "Maybe I'll use it one day." To this day nobody has brought me breakfast in bed.

Everyone weighed in on our situation. Tell people you're making a change and they for sure will tell you their opinion. Some friends were skeptical about the move and getting rid of our things.

"So, like, you're just going to toss it all and sit in a tiny RV with your kids? I couldn't do that to my family."

Or the guy from church who said, "It sounds like a disaster waiting to happen."

Be warned, if you ever take on the task of downsizing from 1700 square feet to 375 - downsizing is therapy on steroids. Your issues will arise from nowhere with a grand entrance. All the things you've carefully shoved away, hoping nobody would ever see, while praying you would never actually have to deal with them. I learned to declutter is the place to start any transformation, and even more than that - our things shouldn't define us - but they do. Each item we keep tells a story. Some are precious items carefully kept, used well, and dearly loved. Other things are reminders of our shortcomings. The endless half-done projects still waiting to be finished. The jeans from 10 years ago we can't button. The stack of unopened mail and papers we need to file.

All of these are disappointing reminders of our failures. We know these things because when we see them, we feel defeat - every time we walk by. Why do we keep this stuff when it makes us feel so lousy? Would we keep seeing a friend who consistently made us feel insufficient and worthless? Of course not. But we are doing the same thing by keeping stuff we don't need anymore. I noticed the thoughts I felt about my home - overwhelm, unmet expectations, and always coming up short - were eerily similar to the thoughts I hold about my calendars, my checkbook, and myself. And sadly, my spiritual life. Overwhelm, unmet expectations, and always coming up short. Maybe the saying is true. How we do anything is how we do everything. These things, my home, calendar, and checkbook, are outward reflections of what's on the inside. It's all connected. And so, as I decluttered my life, I decided to declutter my spiritual closet and the emotional drawers I have stuffed in an effort to ignore the fact I was failing at faith and religion and God.

In the same realization that an overflowing craft closet doesn't make me a good mom, I saw that my overflowing dogma and theology wasn't getting me closer to God. It was easy to see the things I was keeping for my fantasy-self with my physical stuff, but the spiritual stuff was more challenging. For my entire life, I have collected ideas on the world, and God, and how this puzzle fits together. It has not been a pretty process. I know that when organizing a room, it usually gets messier before it gets better. Everything is torn apart, splayed across the floor, and waits on its fate. Each item gets held up. Toss or keep. Toss or keep. Toss or keep.

By this point, I had already started pulling apart my theology, or deconstruction as some call it. This spiritual decluttering ignited a deep feeling of scarcity for me — atonement, science, miracles, prayer, and life after death. I keep my thoughts to myself because there were days I couldn't even say the name Jesus without stuttering, and my girlfriends confidently wore shirts that said, "Just Coffee and Jesus."

If I nixed my beliefs, what would be left? Would there be anything left? Would it change my relationships? What would my husband think? Would I still be able to attend church or even call myself a Christian? I already feel disconnected, so would allowing myself to ride this out leave me even more lonely? Or should I put all these things back into place because of Justin Case?

Once you start this journey, it's hard to stop. I was going full speed uphill and hoping there were tracks on the other side. I kept asking questions, even when it felt dangerous. Who was God before all the clutter of theology and religious opinions? I thought spiritual decluttering would leave me sitting alone in an empty white room, with nothing and no one, but it hasn't yet. The longer I spend sorting it out, the more I've learned questions aren't a path to scarcity but the force magnet for a sacred life. Questions don't lead to scarcity. Questions lead to abundance.

26. Downsizing Comfort

If you aren't in over your head,
how do you know how tall you are?
-T.S. Eliot

By Saint Patrick's Day, we were ready to move into the RV. Boy, did it start off rocky. The babysitter I had scheduled to watch Ethan was a no-show. I tried to call her a few times but got nothing. Ethan was touching everything a two-year-old would, including all the RV buttons we hadn't yet childproofed and still didn't know what they did. I nearly lost it when the slide started closing in on me as I unpacked dishes. I couldn't work like this. I strapped him into his car seat and drove around, trying to figure out what to do. I called my friend Sally.

"Bring him over," she said.

"I'm already in your driveway," I confessed.

After moving most of our things into the RV, we spent the rest of the weekend cleaning out the house and making more trips to donation, storage, or the dump. Two days later, we were wearisome, but all moved in and ready to start a two week trip to San Francisco.

Our very first day started with a morning visit to the emergency room for Evan, and everything fell like dominos from there. The water heater pilot wasn't lighting, and I couldn't get the furnace to turn on, and it was cold and pouring rain outside. I nearly lost it when after running only three loads of laundry, the washer stopped working. And because of all this drama, we were running late for our reservations to see Alcatraz.

People had warned me when buying a new RV there would be kinks. It's why we purchased the extended warranty. But at the moment, I was questioning our decision. Maybe everyone was right. What the heck did we get ourselves into? When we contemplated making this change for our family, it seemed like a good idea, but now I wasn't so sure. We pretty much went all in. We bought this rig and a truck to start a new adventure, but these obstacles had me questioning why we started this in the first place. *Why did we do this?* It would be easy to pretend it was a perfect and smooth transition, but that kind of thinking is what got me into this mess. Pretending to be something I'm not.

We did this because we were restless, and we knew there was something better for us. I was overwhelmed, yet numb and indifferent. I was going through the motions day-in-day-out trying to make my life look like it was supposed to and fell into the trap of conformity without even realizing the life I was chasing wasn't my idea or my ideal. We picked a new life and fiercely ran towards it with only a vague idea of how it was going to look, yet fully expecting it to be a painless transition.

Wake up call. How brash of me to think change should be easy! Change has never promised to be smooth. It's always going to be prickly and uncomfortable, and it's what I asked for without realizing it because uncomplicated isn't the goal. What I wanted was a life full of love, energy, and passion. To be present and alert and to feel it all. The good and the bad. To not live numb. To be pulled and pushed into a new way of being. To be hollowed out and filled up. To see and savor. To be not just aware but affected. To consider my space, your space, and the Creator's space.

I remembered that Martin Luther King Jr. said, "Our very survival depends on our ability to stay awake, to adjust to new ideas, to remain vigilant and to face the challenge of change." I realized I'm indebted to the hurdles because that means growth, and I let all the feelings wash over me. I reminded myself that a life worth living is hard-fought.

I talked myself off the ledge, and we walked to a hole-in-the-wall diner in the cute little beach town of Pacifica. Later we called the RV manufacturer, and a technician came out. He fixed the water heater pilot. I'm embarrassed to admit that both the furnace and washer were not broken, but I was using them wrong. There is such a learning curve to RVing. We lost our tickets to Alcatraz but learned a few valuable things. We took the boys to the San Francisco Zoo instead - which they loved. We left the next day to boondocks in Bodega Bay. We walked lush trails on the coast, which was serene, minus the stress of keeping the boys away from the cliff. They fed pigeons, and we had lunch at the crab shack. We returned to the RV after exploring, and I felt lost because nothing was pressing for me to do. No laundry. No dishes. No house cleaning or yard work. We made smores and put the boys to bed. Jeff and I spent the evening on our patio, holding wine and overlooking the water.

27. Quit Hiding

One of the joys of little kids and motherhood, and military husbands who get called away for the month, is the threat of head lice. I wouldn't call myself a hypochondriac, but if you even so much as mention the word "lice" around my children, I will throw myself on the ground and pitch a fit. I can't deal. It's one of the reasons I have diligently kept my boys' heads shaved. But when you have kids, it will likely happen. On this day, I picked the boys up from preschool and noticed the teachers were wearing plastic gloves, the first sign. Next, all the kid's blankets were in trash bags. Finally, I saw a sign posted on the door. The teachers told me they didn't see any in my boy's hair, but just in case I quickly grabbed my kids, keeping them at a lengthy distance from me, and loaded them into the car. Then the itching started. I couldn't stop. I got back to our RV, doused my head with tea tree oil, and called my friend Michelle.

You know you have a ride-or-die friend when she shows up right away, with a lice comb, and spends an hour raking through your head. Thankfully, no lice. To show my appreciation, I took her out to one of our favorite places for cider and pie. After about an hour, Michelle had to leave, but I stayed to work a little bit. I opened my computer and was having trouble getting the wi-fi to connect. I asked the young guy working behind the counter for help. He was polite and started around my computer to make sure I was looking for the right connection. It was at this moment I became aware of the display on my screen desktop. At the time, I was working through the Brené and Glennon class and also listening to Geneen Roth's audiobook, *Women, Food & God*. I had copious virtual sticky notes all over my desktop. As he's leaning over me, I notice all my notes open. Not limited to:

"I don't want to fail again."

"Shame is eroding my courage."

And Geneen Roth's famous, "We don't want to EAT hot fudge sundaes as much as we want our lives to BE hot fudge sundaes."

Next to that was a sticky note with my current weight number and a quote about how I'd rather meet Oprah than eat a cookie. And then a message popped up from my husband, revealing all the sexy-sexy text messages I had sent him the night before. My face turned fifty shades of red, and I started frantically banging on my keyboard, trying to shut it all down. My voice was shaky as I thanked him for his help and mourned the loss of my favorite pie place, as I could never show my face there again. And now my life was over because is there life without a pie place? I don't think so. My God, I needed to reread Geneen's book.

Maybe he didn't see anything? But I knew it was wishful thinking. But what if he did? What if he saw all my crazy? I sent a message to my life coach, Brooke Castillo.

She replied, "You have no idea what this guy thinks. He might think you are AMAZING for working on yourself. He might be jealous of your sexy talks. (All equally plausible.) But even if he does think you're crazy. HE'S RIGHT. We are totally crazy ...loving it. Have nothing to hide from anyone. That is true freedom. You are working on your weight, and you are working on your mind. HELL YEAH YOU ARE."

She was right. A personal goal of mine is to be the same person publicly and privately, to not feel I'm hiding or embarrassed of who I am, which is hard when I'm still working through it all. I've spent much of my life hiding, trying to be this for one person and that for another. They say the greatest prison is worrying about what others think of you. And I find it ironic that the word origin for *hell* in Old English is "one who covers up or hides something."

Sometimes during my spiritual crisis, I tell myself I'll be okay with people seeing me when I get to the place where I know exactly who I am, and how to articulate it so well, that it doesn't allow for embarrassment, criticism or feedback — the place where I never feel weak or vulnerable. But I've learned that in the absence of these feelings is complacency and apatheticness. My ability to meaningfully connect with others lies in whether or not I can access my vulnerabilities and embrace all parts of myself, including the weakness. Once we accept this, we grow into our next best self. One of my favorite quotes is by Alain de Bottom, "Anyone who isn't embarrassed of who they were last year probably isn't learning enough."

Since I can't avoid embarrassment, maybe I should embrace it as a sign of growth and receive this triggered feeling as a warning to stop recreating the past and start writing a new future.

When I'm not hiding out of embarrassment, I'm shielding myself from criticism. But thanks to the internet, everyone has an opinion, and we all get to hear it. Be it about our relationships, our religion, our parenting, our weight, our money, or the direction of our kid's car seats. It's never-ending. People can be brutal, and people can be wrong. But why is it so hard to let someone believe something incorrect about us?

"Actually…" is the beginning of anything coming out of my kid's mouth before he tells me I'm wrong. Which I never take

197

personally, because he's four and because I know different. I'm okay with him being wrong, and I don't feel the need to correct him. But when someone else believes something wrong about me, it takes everything in me not to say, "Actually..." Why is it so hard to let people be wrong about me? My goals: don't correct them. Don't over-explain my choice, position, or beliefs. Don't try to convince them I'm right. After all, I might not be.

A crappy thing about being a person is our lack of ability to control others' thoughts. It's terrible, but we can't. I should know. I've tried endlessly. I wear black, so I look skinnier. I have a kinder mothering voice in public. I hide the fact that we sometimes drive through McDonald's for dinner. Or that Netflix routinely asks me if I'm still watching. Not only do I try to manage what people think about me, but I try to control what they think about my family. I want people to believe that my kids are well behaved and sweet and that Jeff and I never let the sun go down still upset, but people will think what they want, and people will judge. I hate this. Bottom line, I want them to like me because it feels good. Unconsciously, I even try to win people over I don't like or respect. It's insane. It's addicting, these little shots of approval. But like a slice of my favorite chocolate cream pie, it only feels good in the moment — a quick sugar high and ultimately a crash of exhaustion.

Hiding or in full view, there will be people who don't like me. At least with the latter, I can sleep at night knowing I'm living my truth. It's a myth that by hiding, I can avoid criticism and hold on to my power. I tell myself if they don't see my weakness, they can't use it over me. But hiding is handing over my power. Their judgments cannot break me unless I choose to believe them about myself. Thus I hold my power by letting go of what others think about me.

Our worthiness is not in others' opinions of us. Their opinions are a reflection of who they are. Anaïs Nin said, "We don't see things as they are. We see them as we are." If people are withholding approval of me, at their core, they are withholding approval of themselves. It's the same when we judge them.

The saddest part of all the precious time spent worrying about what others think about me is that I tell myself it's well-intentioned. I'm doing this to protect them. So I don't offend them, or scare them off. As if they won't be able to handle knowing that I'm working on myself. But at the base of my good intentions is the idea that my faults are insulting to people. Maybe they are. But I love my friends for their flaws as much as their strengths. Because it shows their humanity, their realness, and that life isn't spotless.

After Paulo Coelho, author of *The Alchemist*, was released from a mental institution, he realized first, he could never be president because people would find out he was in a mental institution, and second, "I'm crazy. So I can do anything I want." My new mantra: embrace the crazy.

I did learn a valuable lesson, though from showing my computer screen to pie boy. And when I used my computer publicly again, this time for a presentation in front of forty church ladies, I closed all my notes and turned off my message notifications just in the nick of time before I got a popup message from one of my best friends asking if I've ever tried anal bleaching. Which I haven't, because you want to put bleach where? But the church ladies didn't need to know all that.

28. Downsizing Permission

On a sweltering summer day, we took the boys to the local fair. We spent most of the time in long lines, and the boys took turns melting down. I hadn't been to a fair in years, and now as a millennial mom living in a tiny home, I had all kinds of thoughts running through my head. Most were the normal mom kind of worries. *Are these rides even safe when they take them up and down so often? Why did we pay to get into the fair, but still have to buy tickets for every single thing? Where is the healthy food? Where are the funnel cakes? Why do we spend $25 trying to win a cheap stuffed animal? Were these made by sweat-shop children in a third-world country? Would they get tossed aside ten minutes after we get home?* That thought bothered me - until a new situation replaced it. Evan had played the beanbag toss and won a goldfish.

I flashed back to a childhood trip to the county fair. I remember arguing with my mom about playing any game that gave away fish. She was adamant about us not bringing home any animal, fish or otherwise, because, "We are not animal people." This was the phrase she repeatedly expressed anytime we started asking for a pet. "We are not animal people."

But here we were — goldfish in my son's hands. There was no fish food provided, just a single goldfish, in a plastic blue fish tank. Evan was so proud. Water sloshed all over as he carried the tank to the car and announced the fish would be called Umi Tiger. How Evan came up with this name, I will never know. I immediately regretted letting him play the game to win the fish for reasons including animal cruelty, my ignorance on how to take care of a fish, and the larger, err smaller, problem of 375 square feet. We had no space for it. In no uncertain terms, did I want this fish. I told my husband that we could not be fish people. And it hit me. Sweet baby Jesus, I'm turning into my mother.

Growing up, my mom kept a spotless house. From kindergarten to high school, I never had a pet until I was sixteen. I had been pleading for a dog for quite some time. My requests were met with, "We are not animal people." I stopped looking for a dog. But it just so happened that one found me, as dogs often do. My friend, Melanie, and I were jogging in our neighborhood when we spotted an injured animal limping across the street. It looked like a hairless cat, but as we slowly got closer, we realized it was a dog with a horrific mange infection. There was no way this dog would survive on her own. We coaxed the dog to follow us back to Melanie's house, which was closer than my house, and also because her mom loved animals. When we arrived, Melanie's mom quickly grabbed an old towel and started doctoring up the dog. I wanted to keep her but was nervous to ask my mom because I know that we are not animal people. I dialed my mom and begged her to let me keep Molly.

My mom was confused. "Who's Molly?" Followed by, "You *named* her? You never name a stray!" Finally, she cracked, "Fine, but this will be an outside dog only, Angela. I don't want her in the house. Okay?"

I agreed. We cleaned the dog, took her to the vet for medicine, and then I cautiously brought her home.

My mom, who is not an animal person, took one look at Molly, pulled her from my arms, and, affectionately announced, "Oh, she can't be outside. She's an inside dog, for sure." My mom went on to warn me that she wasn't allowed on the furniture.

Again I agreed. But that was the end of *my dog*, Molly, because she instantly became *my mom's dog*, Molly. And even though we weren't animal people, she bonded fast to Molly. They had a special connection, and it didn't surprise me in the least to come home from my job and find Molly on the furniture, curled up with my mom, and that's where Molly stayed for the next 17 years. And just like that, my mom became an animal person.

The one thing I know for sure is that people are allowed to change their minds, their position, their career path, or their thoughts about the world. Words like *never* should be excommunicated from our vocabulary, because except in rare cases, never puts false absolutes on us, making change seem irreverent when it's needed. Nearly every time I've said never, the magic carpet gets yanked from under my words, and I fall.

I'd *never* be so weak to be in an abusive relationship.
I'll *never* fall in love after divorce and get married again.
That family relationship will *never* heal.
I'll *never* have anything in common with her.
I'll *never* feel connected to God again.
I'll *never* feel whole.

Never promotes stagnation and mocks the idea of change, but this should not be. Our lives should be an endless account of flamboyant transformations and modifications: hard-earned advancements and unrefined about-faces. Not old episodes stuck forever on repeat. I know all of this and still have trouble permitting myself to change my mind about God, theology, and the church. For one, it has been so ingrained into the fabric of who I am. Christian church. Christian high school. Christian job. Christian friends. Second, I don't want to let anyone down. More honestly, I don't want them to be disappointed in me. Finally, changing catapults me into an unavoidable predicament of awkwardness, that inevitable scary part.

My 33rd birthday was coming up — one year older and a bit more seasoned. A little more tested and toughened. Unpolished but still refining. I set a goal for myself to be able to sit in discomfort and not run. My heart tells me this is the only way to grow, by willfully coming undone. My friend Ashley captured an image of a brand new butterfly, just out of the cocoon, still unfolding her wrinkled wings. The new butterfly seemed a little klutzy and callow as she moved from the cocoon, a home she formed for herself to keep safe, but now she must shed to fly. The cocoon season wasn't confinement, but an incubator and a safe place where she must completely liquefy before being transformed. A birthplace for new things and she will emerge never to be a caterpillar again.

Because I can be klutzy and ungraceful, the idea that something so beautiful like a butterfly would also be awkward and klutzy, well, it gives me hope and teaches me sometimes the things we once needed for strength and safety, we might not need anymore. Leaving a place where we are enveloped in protection and warmth isn't always smooth, yet one cannot fly still in a cocoon. The process of change, like this newborn butterfly, it's crinkly and unsophisticated.

I think a lot of times, I try something new, and at the first sign of discomfort, I shrink and question. I look at the newness and wrinkles and think I'm doing it wrong. Only wrinkled is not the same as wilted. Wrinkled means you're doing something right and allowing the process of renewal and transformation to happen. How do I move past the awkwardness and permit myself to change? Trina Paulus

204

wrote, "How does one become a butterfly? They have to want to learn to fly so much that you are willing to give up being a caterpillar."

For the awkwardness, I take a little bit of comfort in knowing that even the most accomplished women of our time have self-doubt or insecurities. Maya Angelou described her younger self as "a too-big Negro girl, with nappy black hair, broad feet, and a space between her teeth that would hold a number-two pencil." Julia Child's self-description, as she and her husband Paul got off the ship in France, "I was a six-foot-two-inch, thirty-six-year-old, rather loud and unserious Californian." I'm not the only one who has been grateful to these women, and so many other change-makers didn't let their perceived awkwardness get in the way of making a big impression on the world.

But for the permission to change, this is harder. I am painfully aware of how much time I've spent waiting for people to notice and see my heart, my value, and my worth. Idling quietly in hopes others will offer me their stamp of approval of my change. Although I'm hesitant, I must let go of needing endorsement. I must quit waiting for others to get on board. Most don't even know I want their permission. They love rooting for me and would be supportive, that is, if I could be courageous enough to give them a chance. But they don't know I need it. They're not mind-readers. Maybe I should tell them.

The second group is more tricky. People in the second group might never understand my ways, let alone give me affirmation. They might never get me. If this is the case, am I willing to wait forever? It's taken me long enough to get on board with my own plans. I don't have time to convince someone else. So many times, I've been silent while waiting for 100% clarity on the next step. I reasoned that if I had 100% clarity about my plan, then everyone else will see it too. Or it wouldn't matter what they thought because I was 100% sure. But I know now, few people are lucky enough to be 100% sure of their plan. Most of us fall in the 99% that will never be entirely sure but have to leap anyway. I've heard that terrifying leap is called courage. And in a fascinating and enchanted way, when we stop waiting for others to get on board, we free others to do the same.

29. Downsizing My Heroes

*"Don't spend time beating on a wall,
hoping to transform it into a door."*
- Coco Chanel

I'm a *Pinterest* girl. I have dozens of boards full of things I want to try, styles I like, and quotes that move me. One of my favorites is Coco Chanel: "Beauty begins the moment you decide to be yourself." Who doesn't like a good Coco Chanel quote? She's one of the most revered women in fashion and entrepreneurship. But boy was I ever shocked when I read the book *Mademoiselle: Coco Chanel and the Pulse of History.* The book had a different view on Chanel than I'd ever heard before. I learned her first business was funded by an affair she had with a married man. She was actually known for having several relationships with married men for the sport of it. In an odd twist, she'd aim to befriend the wives of her lovers and also made it her mission to sleep with the husbands of all her best friends. For business purposes, she aligned herself with the Nazis, and as retribution for her body insecurities and boyish figure, she refused to design clothes for curvy women. As a pretty voluptuous gal, or a bigger girl as one bride has said, I take offense to this. But people still quote Coco Chanel, and Pinterest pretends she was a fabulous role model, and now I slightly cringe when I see her quotes. There was a pseudo lesson I learned from this. Don't meet your heroes. Don't read their books. Don't try to learn anything of value about them. Because you'll likely be thoroughly disappointed with the truth like I was and thus began the unraveling of Coco Chanel as someone I revered and applauded as a business icon. Since gaining this new knowledge, my view of Coco has forever changed.

Coco Chanel would have wildly condemned my new RV fashion. If I'm generous, my closet was three feet by three feet for all my hanging clothes. Underneath, I had two drawers for undies, socks, and the like. Gone was the luxury of trying on everything and throwing it on the bed only to relocate it all over to a chair later that evening. There was no space for it. What came out must be put away. Another unglamorous difference in RV life was getting ready - showering, doing my hair and makeup, and getting dressed, it wasn't a solo event anymore. Unlike in a house, I couldn't have Jeff watch the kids while I went upstairs and locked them out of my bedroom to shower in peace. Yes, I could lock the RV bedroom door, but in the tiny space, the raucous from the boys playing, crying, and all else, well, it sounded like they were right under my feet.

We were discovering there were many less-than-charming sides of RV living beyond bad internet and no garbage disposal. There was limited hot water, so even though we had a bathtub, it would chill before it could fill up all the way. There were power outages, and also we'd have to manage our usage of electricity. For example, I couldn't run a load in the dryer, pop my coffee in the microwave, and blow dry my hair at the same time, or the circuit breaker would blow. This happened too many times to count.

Our RV was nice and had a separate air conditioning in each of the three main areas, but only two could run simultaneously, and they were so noisy you couldn't listen to the radio or TV. On the colder days, we'd use our propane heater. We'd know when the propane was out when the RV started getting cold, or we couldn't use the stove. Jeff would have to load up the giant propane tanks, as they were too heavy for me to lift, and get them filled at a local U-Haul place.

We learned traveling wasn't as easy as jumping in and driving to our heart's content. Since we were living in the RV full time, we chose a larger rig, but this meant we had to plan better because many national parks wouldn't accept RVs over 32 feet, and the outside parks are more expensive. We had to diligently map out our route so as not to get stuck on tight spots, which happened a few times, and the tension is real. Plotting everything out took time, and mostly Jeff did this. This wasn't exactly the vision of freedom we thought, and we wondered if we should have chosen a smaller rig.

When it came time to park the RV, I'd have to get out, move the picnic table, and direct Jeff back into the spot while simultaneously trying to keep the kids from crying long enough to park the damn thing. Then, Jeff had to set up while I organized the inside and handled the kids. For sure, I got the better end of the deal. Because the way our RV was built, he'd have to climb partially under the carriage to connect the water and sewage. It was a dirty, literally crappy job, and Jeff found out quickly he didn't enjoy being in charge of the black tank.

Easter weekend arrived along with the endless row of Easter photos on my social media feed. Cute bow ties and frilly dresses and the incessant configuration of families wearing pastels.

My dear friend Sally messaged me, "Do you think all those mothers posting sweet little Easter events with their kids are really having fun? Or are they just the Christmas card people?" Love her.

If they are anything like me, they have passed the exhaustion phase of motherhood, although the exhaustion is never entirely gone, and mutated into a giant mom robot permanently stuck on holiday mode after shopping for basket fillers, setting out Sunday outfits, and prepping the perfect Easter brunch while still making it to the church on time. Because you know if you're late to church on Easter Sunday, the parking lot will resemble *Fight Club*. I have no time for this because I am so very cranky after wrestling little ones into their nicest outfits and exerting all my energy trying to keep their sticky hands off my dress. And the photo, the one I want taken so I can post it on *Facebook* alongside everyone else's, well, it is the least they can do after I used everything - everything - to get us here dressed and alive, and damn it, they owe it to me. *Hold still and smile at the camera.* Plus, I will use these photos later as proof of their perfect childhood.

This year we decided to skip town. To avoid Easter outfits and church celebrations. But this isn't new. As much as possible, I've avoided church on Easter for the last decade. For several reasons. Not limited to my spiritual crisis and avoiding the masses who attend church only on Easter and Christmas, creating the aforementioned fight club in the parking lot. Mostly, I'm unsure about how Sunday school will teach about the death of Jesus. In the days leading up to Easter, I always see videos on social media, usually created by megachurches, with adorable children in adorable Bible costumes, telling the adorable story of Jesus being brutally murdered. All with the lightness of a playful Dr. Seuss book. I'm bewildered at what is made of this atrocity. Because if Jesus' death is something we believed happened, then how irreverent to make it so precious and cute and share it alongside the Charlie Bit Me video. Why doesn't this bother more church people? There is so much I don't get.

After moving into the RV, we tried to leave town as much as possible. For the weekends, when we had to stay local, we would attend church on Sunday. We used the move as an opportunity to try a new church. It was a Foursquare church, and the building had all the nostalgia that an older church building would bring to someone who grew up in the church. From the classrooms to the church kitchen with its mismatched pots and pans, it had all the vibes of a good home church. And when the children were led into the sanctuary to sing an off-key song about God, my heart melted. A Bible study was starting about the Old Testament. I called the office to ask if there was childcare, which there was not. She said if I signed up, they would be sure to get it, and they did. They got childcare just for me to attend. It was a genuine and welcoming church.

On the first Sunday, a woman preached the sermon. It got me thinking about how long it had been since I had seen a female preacher. I couldn't remember, it had been so long. While sitting in the church pew, I messaged my friend Michelle from our former church. "They let women speak here," I told her. Some of our past churches never came right out and said it, but they believed preaching was a man's job. Women are allowed to teach, but only to other women. Teaching on Sunday is not an option because men are in attendance. But at this new church, they let women speak, and I was wearily impressed.

Later that week, I came across a blog post by Kathy Escobar titled "We let women lead…" She points at our acceptance of progress for women when we say things like "We let women lead" - the almost exact phrase I messaged my friend about our new church. Ouch. Yes, progress is good, but underneath this short phrase of "letting women lead" is the more significant assumption that men *allow* women to do certain things. These statements pose as liberating for women, but, as Kathy says, "…does not heal the deep grooves of patriarchy but actually magnifies them." Just when I felt progressively hopeful, I uncovered another level, deeply ingrained in my thinking that suppresses women.

A female friend of mine wants to preach at the church where her husband is a pastor, but she knows better than to ask. Her husband is totally on board, but the church elders, who write his checks, are against it. For him, it's speaking up and losing his job or feeding his family. Beth Moore, perhaps one of the most loved and respected female leaders, recently opened up about her experience being a female leader in today's church. She writes:

> "As a woman leader in the conservative Evangelical world, I learned early to show constant pronounced deference – not just proper respect which I was glad to show – to male leaders and, when placed in situations to serve alongside them, to do so apologetically."

It got me wondering if women were created in the likeness of God, just like men, why in the church do we only use the male pronoun for God. A few times in my writing, I've used the term "She" for God and have been quickly rejected and warned by others that God is in no way a woman. Movies like *The Shack* have been disparaged as false teaching, though it's a metaphor, not teaching. Either way, for some God, is always He. Him. Father. Even though many verses are sharing the feminine qualities of God. A pastor friend was making this point to his church and had people come up after to argue that God is a man. Which makes me wonder why it's so crucial for people to think that God is walking around, package complete with male parts.

Like my inability to ignore the true nature of Coco Chanel, I could no longer ignore the true nature of an unbiased God. My view of God as male unraveled. I started noticing all the "He/Him/Father" used in church, and like the heretic I am, I would mentally swap them with "She/Her/Mother." This small change felt strange at first, but I was living dangerously and playing with a new side of God. One Sunday, I was silently singing Amazing Grace, "And like a flood *Her* Mercy reigns, unending love, amazing grace." Immediately I had a vision of my mom, getting up in the middle of the night, as she often did, to help me. Anything I was going through, bad dreams, illness, or need to talk, it didn't matter what time, she was up helping me in the most gracious, selfless way of only a mother. This idea of God as mother left me breathless and started to fill a void left from the overreaching patriarchy in church. As I reclaimed this feminine tenderness of God, it filled me up with joy and wonder and felt beautiful. This small shift forever changed my view of God, and the nature of God, and was a welcome respite for me.

30. Stop Bringing it Home

Living in such close quarters forced us to get outside more, which was my hope. When we were in the big house, leaving with kids always felt like a monumental task, getting everyone packed and ready. Not to mention the nagging guilt of something else that needed to be cleaned or fixed at home. When we were too tired to leave, we sat numbly on the sofa in complete exhaustion.

Now, we had less to care for in our tiny home. Cleaning the RV top to bottom took less than twenty minutes. So we left the RV to explore and did a lot more hiking, swimming, and visiting the tiny local children's museum. The boys climbed trees, dirt piles, and raced their scooters. We dragged the boys' bikes to trails and the sand buckets to the beach. And then we came back to our tiny home and barbecued and watched family movies. Despite the pitfalls of RV life, having fun felt like proof that we had made the right decision to give up the normal, and that letting go can lead to abundance.

Cutting the ball-and-chain of a house allowed us to enjoy the time we had left in this area of California. The idea that we could hate a place in one situation and love it in another is a good lesson on not just perspective, but the power to make a change. It also taught us to be diligent about what we brought home. I stayed away from Home Goods and Target. With only 375 square feet, I couldn't just bring anything home. I had to plan and be diligent about every inch of space. I had to be fully aware of what was in my house and its purpose. I had to understand how to enjoy something without bringing it home. And that not everything I pass by is mine to keep.

In the same way, I had to stop collecting other people's judgments, assumptions, and input. Moreover, I needed to quit trying to manage other people's emotions. It's hard work.

We took a weekend trip to Glass Beach, just south of where we were. As you might imagine, it's filled with breathtaking pieces of colorful sea glass stones. The crazy thing about this beach is that years ago, it was a landfill site crowded with piles and piles of garbage — the dirty odds and ends of peoples' lives. Once the heaps of rummage got too steep, the town would burn it. This fire would transform the trash into the stunning glass we now can see. I heard the ruby red ones are made of pre-1967 car tail lights. My favorites are the brilliant green ones. Every year, thousands of people stop here to visit, and while some come and see, there's a few who can't help but take a piece or two home with them.

A sign is posted warning visitors it is unlawful to remove the glass, and by stealing it, you are depriving all those who come after you from seeing it. It's tempting to see something so lovely and want to bring it home, to keep a little reminder of the beauty for ourselves. I find the idea ironic that we would want to collect someone else's transformed trash to keep as our own. But we do this every day when we compare our lives with the fragments of others. Our struggles. Our bodies. Our beauty. Our bank accounts. Our relationships. We look to social media and see people's lives laid out like glass on the beach. Their unique experiences and ideas they've toiled and burned until it looks like something acceptable, sitting side-by-side other people's acceptable, dressed up garbage, abet transformed, and we want to have a little part of it for ourselves. We see their beauty as it is now, and not the rubbish it once was. Perhaps we see this while we are still on fire, searing and unsure and blistering within our own conversion. It's hot and sometimes painful. It's hard to remember that at the end of our enkindling is something quite beautiful too, but it only comes with the flames of difficulty and embers of adversity, and we must keep burning.

We must not bring home broken pieces of another person's path. Not everything is ours to bring back. Not every new idea, charity opportunity, and political issue are ours to take home. Not every story or judgment or conclusion is for us. And even if we can adopt them, it doesn't mean we should. Years ago, when I was working as a receptionist at a church, my friend Gina told me, "People will tell you things, but you can't take them with you." I remember nodding that I understood. I wasn't sure what things they would be, but I was sure I wouldn't take them with me. I didn't plan on it, but they snuck in. But this would become clearer to me when I ran out of space.

A good lesson in this happened at the beginning of my second marriage. Jeff and I were going home to visit family. Since we lived on the east coast, my family didn't know Jeff very well in the beginning. I wanted them to like him and, because of my past marriage, I wanted them to be confident he was treating me well. The only thing was that Jeff is an *introvert*. And his quietness is a stark contrast to my large and rather loud family. I wanted them to see all his admirable qualities, and I made it my responsibility to facilitate this, which lead to a few awkward moments and the additional stress of overcompensating, all at the task of trying to control what other people think.

But people are going to think what they want, and I'm not responsible for it. I'm learning it's not my job to manage or change them. Other people are responsible for their thoughts and emotions. I

217

can't make others feel a certain way, and trying to control their emotions is manipulative. Emotions come from perception. Even if I try to manage them, and I have, they still interpret and respond in whatever way they see fit according to their perception. And in this way, I decided to stop bringing home other people's emotions. It only leads to more anxiety and an inauthentic relationship, whereas I'm acting one way to try to elicit a particular response from another person, also known as lying.

As I examined these ways, I tried to self-protect, I also noticed I was lumping everyone into a clean, organized basket and giving them the same label: Everyone. *Everyone* thinks I'm scattered. *Everyone* expects me to show up, to volunteer, to raise my kids this way or that way. *Everyone* thinks I should stay quiet. *Everyone* thinks I shouldn't speak against the system.

And during this faith crisis, questioning the beliefs I was raised with, I felt like *everyone* at church was judging me. *Everyone* thinks I'm backsliding. *Everyone* gathers that I have a lesser view of God. *Everyone* thinks I'm wrong. *Everyone* wants me to accept the version of Christianity the church is handing out, without question. *Everyone* is out for the patriarchy. And it turns into *Nobody* understands me.

Everyone. Nobody. Words I for sure needed to retire. I learned the concept sociologists call the "generalized other" - our internalized idea of what we think others think about us. Here's how it often shows up for me; When I hesitate to say something or hide things that are important to me because I'm afraid of what everyone thinks; When I leave an event and replay a particular conversation because I just know they now believe the wrong thing about me; When I'm hesitating to make a decision, hit publish, or speak up about something important to me; When I'm sure others are thinking I'm not doing enough, smart enough, successful enough, put together enough. Where did I get these thoughts? Surely someone must have said them to me. But when I tried to remember who told me these things, I was surprised. Sometimes it was maybe one or two people, and sometimes it was nobody. Sometimes, not a single person had ever said these things to me, and yet I choose to believe they thought them.

I heard the story of a woman in her thirties who was worried about what others thought about her. In her forties, she was too busy to care. And then in her fifties, she realized they weren't even thinking about her.

Why was I giving others such an influential role in my life? I don't want to live my life at the mercy of what just a few people may or may not think about me. I started asking two questions when considering the opinion of others: Is It True? And So What?

Is it true? If the opinion is not true, then I can let them be wrong about me.

But if the judgment is true, then So What? They have an opinion about me, and it's true. So what? What's the big deal with this judgment being correct? What am I making this mean? I'm learning that it's not important if they think something about me, but it's what I think about myself. Ultimately I can't change what others think about me. Trying only leads to pain, I know. I love that Byron Katie says what others think of us is none of our business. What we can change is how we view ourselves. And if we do this with compassion, understanding, and love, it shows others how to see us with the same.

31. Downsizing Filters

If anything can put a sour note on a quick trip to the grocery store, it's wrestling my three-year-old into his car seat. It's a tantrum every single time. His strength doubles as he twists and contorts into the shapes of an acrobat, and I struggle to pull the straps around his shoulders. He ignores all bribes and threats while my ice cream sits melting in the summer heat. By the time I click the last buckle, my hair looks like I auditioned for WWE. And nearly every time I have to deadlift one of my boys into their car seat, I think of this 911 call I took years ago.

The line rings. I answer in my most professional operator voice, "9-1-1, what's the location of your emergency?"

An out of breath woman yelps back. "There was a Mom. Who just (static) threw her kid out of her car. I mean, the car was still moving. She tossed him. He looked young, like maybe two." She paused to take a breath. "She got out of the vehicle, picked the kid off the ground, and put him back in the car. Then she just drove off. She just drove off!"

The reporting woman didn't want to stay on the scene, and by the time the officers arrived, there was no evidence of anything having happened, but a little more investigation found the truth along with the mom and boy at the hospital. The mom never threw her son from the car. He was four years old and refused to get into the car.

So the mom said, "Get into this car right now, or I'm going to leave you here."

And who hasn't threatened to leave their child? It was right out of the old Desperate Housewives episode when Lynette's boys are acting up. She threatens to leave them, pretends to drive off, but really is circling, and when she comes back, they've made friends with Karen McCluskey and gone inside her home for lemonade, leaving Lynette freaking out, wondering where her boys went. This was basically the same situation, with only slight differences. It went like this:

"Get in the car," she demanded. "We're going to be late!"

The boy yelled with conviction, "No.".

"Fine. I'm leaving. If you want to come with me, get in the car."

The boy throws himself on the ground. "NO."

Then the tired mother pretends to drive off, and just as she slightly pulls away from the curb, the kid ran and jumped on the slow-moving car and bounced off onto the sidewalk. This was the point the 911 caller witnessed. Thankfully the kid was okay. Not even a hair out of place, but the mom still took him to be looked over. The caller got most of the details wrong. The child wasn't two; he was four. The mom didn't throw him; he jumped on the car. Was she lying? I don't think so. I think this was how she witnessed it. The way her brain interpreted the portion of the event she saw.

Most people under stress don't hear the first 10 seconds of what you tell them. Which is why, a good chunk of the time, when I would say, "9-1-1, what's the location of your emergency?" people responded with, "Ahh, Hello? Is this 9-1-1?" The stress of their situation caused them to miss critical things said. It's not their fault. It's hard-wired in us. We often can easily see this in others. But I couldn't tell you how often I miss critical things said because I can't see them. It's sometimes impossible to move beyond ourselves and to see anything different beyond the lifetime of filters we have fostered in our lives.

If you have ever heard a six-years-old give his perfect option about Bernie Sanders, you don't say the child has developed a clear view of politics. You say, "Wow, I know what his parents think of Bernie Sanders," because it's so apparent the opinion wasn't his but likely his parents. We collect and accumulate ideas about relationships, money, and God. We have filters for how we see our parenting strategies or how far we stand behind someone in the line at Starbucks. We are so deep into our filters. It's easy to overlook an entire world of people who have different filters and who do things differently than us because we don't see there is another way. In relationships, not being able to acknowledge, tame, and move beyond our filters causes us to miss critical things said. Filters are like green ivy growing up from the ground; untamed filters weave slowly around our legs, to our core, and wrap tightly around our hearts suffocating us.

Unfortunately, I am not immune. I have filters for how I want to raise my kids, what my body should look like, which morning news channel I watch, and what my relationship with God looks like. I hold these filters. I nurture them. I defend them. More than anything, they need to be protected because I've placed my identity and my ego in them, not realizing that most of my filters are a reflection of the cultural nuisances around me, just like the Bernie Sanders boy.

A few years ago, President Jimmy Carter publicly resigned from the Southern Baptist Convention after six decades. He wrote in an article that his decision was sealed when "The convention's leaders, quoting a few carefully selected Bible verses and claiming that Eve was created second to Adam and was responsible for original sin, ordained that women must be "subservient" to their husbands and prohibited from serving as deacons, pastors or chaplains in the military service."

My mother-in-law shared this article, and a friend of hers made a comment that started with, "I cannot help but see God wouldn't want women to lead..."

The problem, among others, is the phrase "I cannot help but see." It wasn't that the commentator was physically, mentally, or intellectually able to see. It was that he had already decided not to see.

This was like my friend, who didn't want to talk bad about the church. She'd already decided that she wouldn't hear otherwise. People want to believe the church is good, so that's how they experience it.

Wrapping my identity in my filters permits me to automatically dismiss ideas that counter my beliefs or twist them to strengthen my position while missing the entire conversation. It's called confirmation bias. And then to prove I'm on the right path, I look for validation from others who've already come to the same conclusion I have. If something doesn't agree with me, I ignore it. It keeps me in my comfort zone. It makes me feel less alone as I attempt to discredit the other side.

> "Our greatest hope of self-correction lies in making sure we are not operating in a hall of mirrors, in which all we see are distorted reflections of our own desires and convictions. We need a few trusted naysayers in our lives, critics who are willing to puncture our protective bubble of self-justifications and yank us back to reality if we veer too far off. This is especially important for people in positions of power." From the book, *Mistakes Were Made (But Not by Me): Why We Justify Foolish Beliefs, Bad*

Decisions, and Hurtful Acts, Caroll Tavris and Elliot Aronson.

The authors tackle why we cling to our wrong choices, causing us to believe stories of our choosing and allowing us to keep the narrative that we are smarter or have chosen the morally superior way but ultimately keeping us stuck in a wrong decision or belief. They named one reason we don't admit mistakes or bias is because we don't want to accept the sunk costs of our choices, and it's easier to find reasons to support them in being correct. Often we are too close to see past our passionate opinions about the situation. As they say, you can't read a label from inside a jar.

I can't see my errors. But it's effortless to see them in others. A while back, I was in the women's only sauna at the gym because my personal workout plan is a trio of the spa, sauna, and coffee bar, while taking advantage of gym daycare. Don't judge me. Anyways, another woman was sitting there in a towel. A third woman walked in wearing bright Victoria Secret's Pink leggings and earbuds, humming softly, and she began stretching post-workout.

The first woman barked at VS girl for bringing her cell phone into the sauna. "You can't have that here. Leave now, or I will tell the front desk."

The VS girl looked wounded and shocked. As she mumbled an apology and slumped out, I asked the woman why it bothered her so much.

Matter-of-factly she replied, "Because cell phones are making people lose their humanity."

We can see when others lose their humanity but not ourselves.

My friend Leslie reminds me, we often judge ourselves by our intentions, but we judge others by their actions. At that moment, it was easy for me to see this and chuckle at the ridiculousness, but then also acknowledge that I don't see it when I do the same. And to have more grace when I see other's errors and shortcomings.

I heard Charles Eisenstein say something like, "In some sense, we are all one. If I were in your situation, then I would do as you do. If I think otherwise, then it means I don't understand your situation." If someone tells you their story and you don't end up with the exact conclusion they did, maybe you didn't hear them. I realize this is a significant overstatement, but the principle behind it gives us a way to strive to have more understanding, empathy, and respect for the choices others make.

Our minds are so conditioned to stay in our comfort zone, making the million-dollar question, how do we move past our conclusions, our tightly held identity, our ego, to create space for different views to be heard and validated as equally valuable as ours? It is tough because our brains get clouded to feed our egos. In the book *Everything Belongs*, Richard Rohr calls the act of removing filters Cleansing the Lense.

"The truth is always too much for our ego. Who is ready for the whole truth? I'm not. For the thinking of the ego is largely based on fear. Fear of what I might not be. Fear of what I might see. Fear I won't be successful or accepted, or that I will be hurt. So we have to recognize how dominant fear is in our lives."

I think how we move past filters and fear, is to become aware of them. The only way to become aware of them is to choose situations where we live outside of them. So often we live in bubbles and miss out on the richness of other areas. For me, traveling and books have been the guiding hand forcing my critical thinking skills and giving me glimpses into someone else's education, choices, and life. The first part is usually the discomfort, sometimes annoyance, but sometimes if I sit with it long enough, it blossoms into acceptance and love.

32. More Downsizing

It was almost New Year's, my most beloved holiday. Three years ago, sparked by a life coach named Susan Hyatt, my dear friend Leslie and I began a New Year's tradition. We live a few thousand miles apart, but we dress up, pour a glass of champagne, and have the most compelling phone call. We recap the last year, month by month, reflecting on the things we accomplished, the things we endured, and the things we created. We state our highs and lows, and we celebrate all the wonderfulness of the last year. Then we "precap" the next year, month by month. We are naming and giving life to the things we will do, create, and offer back to the world. Words are so powerful, and by speaking our dreams and our hearts, I believe we are speaking blessings into our lives. It's the best way to commence a new beginning and reflect on the year we were leaving.

At this point, it had now been nearly ten months of living in the RV. Forty-one weeks since we flipped our lives upside down. Two hundred eighty-seven days since we cut ties with all the things we didn't truly value. Letting go of the physical stuff had freed up mental and emotional space. It allowed me to show up better as a mom. We tried our best to live in the moment and make daily things more fun. I made different music playlists so the boys and I could rock out in the car. Our car dance parties sparked laughter and lightheartedness I'd consistently lose at the peek of kid meltdowns. I learned that I *needed* to laugh like I needed to brush my teeth - daily. We finger painted and jumped in puddles. We spent more time outside, walking and climbing trees and riding bikes. We visited San Francisco, Crescent City, Klamath, Kernville, San Diego, Benbow, Brookings a few times over, and finished off the year with a fantastic trip up the Oregon Coast. We made priceless memories.

Asserting a life around adventure, threw a spotlight on our marriage, specifically, our dating life. As a military family, we move often. And sitters, precious lifelines for those of us with littles, are a luxury hard to come by. I've developed a strategy of poaching the workers at the gym daycare. At first, it was a little awkward having them come to the RV, but it was worth it to make our weekly dates mandatory. Sometimes we would miss a week, and other weeks we went out twice. People ask if this is expensive. Yes, it is, but it is worth every dime. Sitters and dates are not cheap, but it's dear and beautiful to our marriage, our friendship, and my sanity.

As January approached, my excitement for the next year couldn't be contained. We were waiting for military orders sending us who-knows-where. Perhaps my favorite part of being in a military family is moving around. We were hoping to go overseas, but I was okay with pretty much anywhere. Send me to New York or Texas or Florida or back to the PNW. I'm game for anything. Bring. It. On.

Another thing on my precap, that I was both eager and emotional about, was my scheduled breast reduction surgery. I have come to a place of better body acceptance, but for as long as I can remember, I've had issues with the girls. Since I was in fourth grade, I got teased about the size of my breasts. The boys called me milk jugs and laughed as they threw food down my shirt. For over a decade, I've slept in a bra, and even to have my bra off during the time it takes to shower, is painful. I wear two bras to the gym. Three if I'm planning on jogging. And don't get me started on breastfeeding, which resulted in carpal-tunnel from holding my breast not to suffocate my babies. Like coffee, back pain was a part of my everyday life. I tried to ignore it, but as soon as I weaned my offspring, I started looking into getting a reduction. While I loved my girls, I was tired of repositioning each of them back into my bra every time I'd bend over to pick something up off the floor.

Further, I was over expensive bras that resembled FEMA tents and painting tarps at Home Depot, and only came in dull colors like tan, black, and white. So I was downsizing. And like the saying goes, when in Rome for a breast reduction, get a tummy tuck. Or something like that.

I hesitate to tell you all this because of fear of judgment from the body-positive movement people, whom I deeply admire. I've seen the cute memes of post-baby bellies with stretch marks with the quote to be a "tiger who's earned these stripes." I'm proud of my body for producing two perfect babies. I own my body and imperfections, and I felt amazing in my body before I had surgery. Well, mostly, because I'm human. However, my stomach had been badly damaged from having babies, and pregnancy tore open my stomach muscles like the Grand Canyon. Doctors call this diastasis recti. I called it an upside-down kangaroo pouch because I could hide things TSA would never find. But with zero core support and constant back pain, I was desperate for a fix. Plus, my kangaroo pouch would get caught in my jean zipper, which freaking hurts. I downsized everything else up to this point, so why stop now?

I booked a fantastic surgeon in Irvine, and my parents were going to take care of me after my surgery. I was in a *Facebook* group for women getting surgery. Some of the gals were keeping it a secret from their families. I didn't want to keep it a secret, not that I was out advertising it on social media, but I was tired of hiding. It only leads to feelings of shame. Plus, even if I wanted to keep it a secret, my mom had already blabbed it to my entire family, so there's that.

It was amusing having other people weigh in on my body. What I should do. What I shouldn't do. What I should like and accept. What I shouldn't change. Everyone had an opinion, and everyone loved to share it with me. One woman told me she was "anti-vanity surgery." Perfect. One woman told me I should love my body just as it was. I found it interesting that she was assuming I didn't. You can love something and be able to change it at the same time. In fact, I believe the people who hate their bodies before surgery are likely to hate it still after. I'm reminded of the Carl Jung quote, "We cannot change anything until we accept it. Condemnation does not liberate; it oppresses." Nonetheless, my close girlfriends were excited for me.

I scheduled my surgery for the second week in January. As Christmas approached, we smoothly rode through the holidays. I took all the pressure off of myself and did what worked for us. I didn't dress up. I didn't go to dozens of parties. I didn't bake seven different kinds of cookies in my tiny RV oven. It was amazing. Why hadn't I done this sooner? I did crafts with the boys, and we decorated cookies with premade frosting. It was organic frosting, which cancels out the "pre-made" fact. I didn't force gift buying but truly enjoyed giving gifts this year, unlike years past, and I let myself savor the whole season. Most importantly, and like a broken record, I said no over and over again to the things I didn't want to do. It was the most beautiful, fabulous holiday season.

Along with saying no to everything, I also said no to hosting this year's IF:Gathering, but several of the women were bummed and asked me to consider it. We were living in a very remote area, and there aren't a lot of options for women to attend faith-based conferences. The conference would be a month after my surgery. After talking to a few friends, and with their help, I agreed to move forward. I partnered with a few local churches and got everything into place, so when January rolled around, I could focus on my surgery.

I flew to Southern California, only slightly nervous about the surgery and recovery. What if my boobs turned out too small? What if I lost feeling in my nipples? Feeling in my nipples is of high importance to me. It ranks up there with lasagna and country music. To prepare myself, I researched hundreds of breast surgeries. My internet search history during this time was beyond sketchy. After looking at an obscene amount of naked women, for research, my biggest concern was my boobs would be too lopsided or square-ish, like some of the breast reductions I saw. What if I had boobs that looked like Sponge Bob Square Pants? Would I miss my Dolly Parton top half?

I asked my husband, "Are you going to be okay if I have teeny-tiny boobs?"

He joked that he only needed a handful.

For all my worries, I wanted to have the surgery, and I forced my mind to stay positive.

The morning of my surgery, the doctor took a blue marker and small level to my chest and stomach until I resembled a printout from the Richter scale. Then I climbed on to a hospital bed. The anesthesiologist made some corny joke, which I can't recall because he's good at his job, but I remember it made me instantly like him. Before I knew it, I was waking up a few hours later. My sister and parents drove me home, and even though I was awake, my brain was still foggy. I tried to text Jeff that I was okay, but with all the medication, I'm not sure who ended up getting texted or what it said.

The next day I went back to the doctor's office, and when he removed the bandages, I could see my new self for the first time. I was a bit overwhelmed in every way I had hoped. I had a tiny, perfectly rounded top rack (sensation TBD), and my stomach muscles were noticeably zipped up. Back at my parent's house, I rested and took Arnica and Bromelain supplements. I spent 24/7 in my compression garments. I was deeply in debt to whoever invented the toilet seat riser and also my mother, who helped me get up and down for a week. And just like that, my back pain was gone.

A week later, I flew home. I wasn't able to do much around the RV yet, but Jeff was a champ and let me rest. My new normal for the next three weeks was sleeping on our sofa recliner at night. I couldn't run or even stand up straight right away, but I did my best to watch movies and snuggle the boys, in between yelling at them to stop elbowing my stomach as they tried to get comfortable. The kids were so impressed, they told their teacher that mom got a new belly button.

33. Ready to Walk Away

A month after my surgery, I hit a breaking point with the Christian church. I was ready to quit and walk away from it all. It was a Friday afternoon, and I was preparing for the IF:Gathering conference starting later that evening. We had about 85 women coming, and there was much to be done.

This last year had been pretty amazing with all my church issues, and with all my letting go, and with all my work on forgiveness, I felt not only prepared but even excited to gather with women to watch the conference. I craved the fellowship of women and that incredible feeling of a women's gathering. Last year's conference went relatively smoothly, and I mostly expected that for this year. It was going to be better. I could feel it. Well, it was either that or my period and migraine that showed up an hour before we started. I popped a few ibuprofen but received no relief. Like clockwork, at 5:00 pm, my tummy started to swell up, as if I had just inhaled three Chipotle burritos. My doctor told me this could happen for a while after surgery as my body rebuilds my lymphatic system. But the show must go on, Chipotle baby bump and all.

Women shuffled in, hugged each other, and eventually got seated. My friend Michelle made a quick trip back to my RV for the metal Gathering sign I bought for the photo booth. Our lovely friend Julie set up a henna table and started decorating arms with crosses, in purple and brown ink. There was a steady sound of chatter. As the conference was beginning, I walked to the stage to welcome everyone. I thought about the gathering from two years before and the mentions of hell and saving people from eternal damnation, and just in case things would go that way again, I opened with some advice I had heard a few years before. I told the women, "We all come to the table with something, be it our own experiences, education, history, and theology. It's how we hear and see and learn — our filters. Speakers teach based on the things they've learned, but they also have filters that will show up in their teaching. Some of the messages here today might be for you. They might not be. Maybe they are for the woman next to you. It's okay. But the foundation of us being here is our shared love for Jesus. We take the fish and leave the bones. We need to recognize that filters might have been necessary to protect us from something but shouldn't be a permanent part of the way we communicate, and we are going to be communicating a lot this weekend. By truly seeing, understanding, and loving others, we get a truer glimpse at God." I waddled off stage, and the live stream started rolling.

The worship started, but then it abruptly stopped. It happened a few more times. Of the eighty-five women, most hadn't been to a live stream conference before, and many women were looking around puzzled as I ran over to the computer technician to troubleshoot. We learned the problem wasn't on our end, and many other gatherings were having the same issues. The stream started again. Everyone continued to worship, but then it kept stopping and starting. There were more looks of confusion and sounds of chatter. I began to sweat. Finally, we got a good stretch of playtime, and the worship song was hitting home. Women were praying and singing with their hands raised in the dimmed lighting. Then mid-song abrupt silence. We had lost connection again. In the darkroom, you could hear a pin drop.

I ran back towards the IT desk again. Then one by one, the women joined together to sing acapella right where the song had cut off. The beauty of this moment was overwhelming. I drew a sharp breath, and shivers ran up my arms. I was overcome with indescribable peace and love for God and these women. It was this moment, a holy spirit moment, I felt the most profound gratitude for God and life and these women.

The conference ran without any more connection problems. During the next three hours, I only caught glimpses of the speakers because I was moving around the room, making sure everything was okay as we prepared for dinner and such and filtered endless requests and feedback from these women I loved so much. *Can you turn the air up, please? It's freezing in here. I can't hear anything. It's too loud. It's too dark. I can't see my notes. It's so bright, can we turn it down to get the full worship experience?* I love these women.

The last speaker was up. It was Christine Caine, whom I've seen speak over a dozen times, and I've long admired her story and charisma. Most everything she said was on par with the conference, but in the middle of her presentation, she mentioned how Christians believed marriage should be between a man and a woman. The comment was quick but spoken very calculated, as if it was standard for every Christian to feel the same thing about same-sex marriage. Which, clearly, in 2018, we don't. But then, she went on. There was a part about how non-Christians think we are bigots for our beliefs, and we are being persecuted. I stood at the IT desk mouth ajar. Ugh. It sounded like a typical American Christian victim card. I hated it. I once heard someone say the ultimate way for the ego to find power is to prove you are a victim. Christians are not victims here. Not in the United States, and playing the victim card is another way to divide outsiders from the church.

I wanted someone to tell me this wasn't happening again. I muddled through to the end of the evening, hoping the diverse group of women wouldn't have noticed. But they did. As they walked out, a few women expressed it was getting too political. One gal seemed flustered. I was at a loss for words and did my best to apologize. I was the one who'd brought this local gathering, and I felt terrible that women would leave hurt or frustrated again, although I was right there with them.

The conference ended for Friday night, but everyone was going to be back Saturday morning early. I went home that night, trying to process it. On the one hand, I hated people playing the Christian victim card. On the other hand, I deeply admired Caine's work in human trafficking, and I've appreciated hearing her speak before. I needed to gain perspective. The best people I could turn to were the other women running IF:Gatherings in their local communities all over the world. If I was feeling like this, chances are others were. I posted in the leader's *Facebook* group.

"I just wanted to share a few thoughts, and I'm still processing all this, but I was so thrown off by Christine Caine's message and had others express concern to me when the event ended tonight. It's the third IF:Local I've hosted, and I've seen all five years. One of the things I love about IF is its ability to bridge the gap between different denominations and theology while keeping the focus on Jesus. While I loved "endurance is built with pressure and resistance," I didn't feel it was a good idea to throw in a comment about same-sex marriage when it's such a dividing issue in our church right now.

But even more, my real trouble was how much she emphasized Christians as victims in that we live in "a world that thinks we are idiots," and the world is telling us we aren't loving or compassionate. She said Christians are pressured, misunderstood, not included, and categorized as intolerant, bigoted, narrow-minded, dumb, and uneducated.

As I said, I'm still processing all of this, but the whole idea that we are being persecuted or pressured as Christians isn't sitting right with me. Being thrown in jail for believing in Jesus is pressure. Having people not agree with us on theology points should not equal pressure.

It feeds the notion that we, as Christians, are victims. And victims can never, ever lead from a place of fearless love."

I posted this and wasn't sure what to expect. Part of me thought maybe I should keep quiet, but the other part reasoned that two years ago, when someone posted about the dicey hell and salvation talk they were conflicted with, I deeply appreciated knowing I wasn't alone. It meant so much that someone would speak out. I also genuinely wanted to see where the line would be for other people.

I thought I was ready for whatever the responses would be, but I wasn't. I was under no naiveté that everyone would agree with me, that wasn't the point, but I wasn't expecting the amount of backlash from these other Christian women. While some women commented that they understood, maybe even had similar thoughts, many were vocal with disapproval. I took in all the responses.

Some women agreed, saying they wished Caine hadn't spoken as if everyone was in agreeance. Some women said they wished there was more love in what she said or how she said it. Some pointed out their denomination had almost split over the same-sex marriage issue. Some, who were presenting a delayed version of the conference, decided not to show this speaker. Some said it was distracting, and these issues shouldn't be talked about in a "throwaway line." Some people were proud, calling the controversial parts of her message a truth bomb and were happy she was sticking with the Word of God. Others said truth isn't a bomb - it's a person. One gal said she found a two-minute side rant about how Caine felt persecuted for traditionally orthodox Christian beliefs didn't make sense, because the rest of the conference focuses on people who are genuinely persecuted - "especially since the focus wasn't redemption and the hope of the cross but her personal feelings about being tired of being made to feel like a bigot for her beliefs."

Some said she was spot on. And there was the typical, we don't get to decide what sin is, God does, and we speak up because we love them and want them to get right with God. Some applauded her from not shying away from the truth and said acceptance is condemnation, and God's Word is clear, and the speaker was spot on. Some said she was right, that Christians are being treated like idiots and are seen as judgmental and unloving. More people said she was "spot on."

The words "spot on" were used so many times, I looked at my husband and said, "If one more person responds that she was "spot on" I'm going to shit a brick."

There were more "truth in love" comments and also a comment on how it's more painful for us as Christians to have to point out the sin, but it's our job. Wait - it's going to hurt me more than it hurts you? Isn't this what parents in the fifties said before they spanked their kids? Some said it was bold and hard to hear, but, you guessed it, spot on. God, help me.

Some were dismissive, saying it was easy to get caught up in the details, but we shouldn't let a side comment overshadow the main message. Some said they hoped I would have an opportunity to figure out what God was trying to teach me through this. One gal wrote that it must have taken me a really long time to type a comment stating my opinion and that instead, I should be getting on my knees and praying for the prodigals to come home. Some said we need to be aware of where our darts are coming from because sometimes they are self-inflicted by self-absorption and not the bigger picture. My comments are self-absorbed?

Some just high-fived the ones who disagreed with me or commented in all caps, TRUTH. Some said if I actually believe God's word, then I'd understand this is our job regardless of the view of the world. The ones that were especially cutting ended with "praying for you" or "dig deep sister."

Some said that we should give all the speakers freedom to talk about nonessentials in a way we disagree with. Some said we should keep the main thing the main thing. Some pointed to the beauty of the gathering and how there's a variety of voices. Others pointed out that the less conservative speakers from the very first year either weren't invited back or chose not to return. Yes, I did miss them.

One gal said she hadn't watched yet, but her heart was flooded with thankfulness Caine did "go there" and that she didn't think it was off-topic. She. Had. Not. Watched. It.

Some said it was so sad that I was shaming and putting the speaker down and that she was just a Christian standing on truth in a place where we are supposed to be safe and love each other. Hi pot, meet kettle.

One compared my post to the most discouraging moment of her life when someone criticized her. She said my comments were at the wrong time, in the wrong place, and her heart was broken for the women who saw my post who may have been inspired by the conference and the leaders who really needed to hear stories of how God was working. One gal said to another, have a glass of wine, and have less opinions.

Perhaps the most disturbing, to me personally, was the woman from the Poulsbo movie church, who just a few years before had stopped me on my way out of Sunday service to invite me to the mom's group. I wasn't sure if she didn't remember me, or maybe didn't care, but she littered the thread with over the top praise towards all the people who disagreed with me and said they were spot on.

I muddled through the rest of the conference Saturday as these comments kept popping up, but I felt an overwhelming sadness. I tried to remember the words I had just spoken to the group earlier. It was okay if not everything is for us. I tried to remember to take the fish and leave the bones. I tried, but couldn't muster this. Why does the church continue to make me feel like the girl who swings by her ex-boyfriend's place on Tuesday night because she so badly wants to be held, and then hates herself on her Wednesday morning walk of shame?

Over the next two days, I continued to get private Facebook messages from others, trying to prove that American Christians are victims. And a few that offered words of support. Some said they couldn't speak up publicly because of their position.

As I thought about what happened and the responses, I felt shattered once again. Later that week, the thread was taken down after receiving hundreds of comments, and I received a very kind, loving message from the staff at the IF:Gathering. They said they were sorry for any comments that may have hurt me and said I had done nothing wrong, but I felt terrible. I can't say enough how gracious the IF:Gathering team was after all the comments, and I hold a deep appreciation for all the women and men who put the conference on. It's a tremendous amount of work, and I don't doubt their hearts are pure in reaching women for God. But knowing this didn't stop me from coming undone.

I talked to Sally.

She said, "Honey, these are just regular Christian women that happen to speak well. *They can't all be Jen Hatmaker!*"

Still, I could not drag myself to attend church the next Sunday or the one after that. I was spiritually depressed. What was I even doing here? I likely didn't belong with these women. Maybe I didn't belong in church. Perhaps I should have never put on the conference. With all the emphasis on morality and Christian victims, there seemed to be no room for Jesus.

Maybe Caine was right.

Maybe we are not included, because we routinely exclude.

Maybe we are feeling pressure because if others disagree, our evangelical programming tells us to dismiss them as doubters.

Maybe we are misunderstood because we push our views on others instead of trying to understand them.

Maybe the world is telling us we aren't loving or compassionate, because we aren't acting loving or compassionate.

I continued to avoid church on Sunday. A few weeks away turned into a few months, until I felt ready to walk back into the church. As I took my seat during worship after being away, I was embraced by a few women and sat down next to Jeff. Then I realized that it wasn't even women at my church who had said all these things to me, but a group of women I'd never met. The women at my church, whom I knew, were quite loving. It's easier to love in proximity and more comfortable to hate from a keyboard.

I tried to forgive and forget, but I still felt hot with anger. I felt disgusted. I felt contemptuous of the church. I felt taken down. I felt defensive. And then it hit me. My thoughts around the whole thing had me feeling like a victim.

Oh, the irony.

If the first act of war is defensiveness, then I need to work on openness. Humility. Tolerance. Acceptance.

34. Sifting and Waiting

One day after an eye doctor appointment, I met my friend Michelle for coffee - a different Michelle than my pie buddy. We were sipping our lattes and chatting about contemplative prayer. Then she mentioned the Cosmic Christ. And I was all, Cosmic what? I had no idea. What kind of heathenism is this? I grew up in non-denominational churches. A non-denominational church is pretty much a Baptist church, but with a coffee shop and a pastor who wears skinny jeans, pretending to be way less judgy than the Baptists are, but it's just a different paint job. Here I was, my whole life in the church, and still, I had never heard of the Cosmic Christ. My apparent next thought: it must be New Age.

New Age is the catch-all classification to anything that counters deeply rooted church dogma. Anything that is mentioned on Oprah, or anything that refers to God as The Universe, or anything that pushes the predetermined evangelical comfort zone, can safely be squared up as New Age. I've spent hours asking my Christian friends what would make an idea or thought about God be considered New Age. I've asked them to define New Age. None of them know. I find this amusing that such a hard line is drawn for these New Age ideas that we are too disposed of, but nobody knows what it is.

So when Michelle mentioned Cosmic Christ, I lovingly thought she was off her rocker, but I looked into it and found an audiobook by Richard Rohr. While running errands and preschool drop-offs, I cried my way through his audiobook *Falling Upward.* He divides life into two halves, not by age but by spiritual experience. The first half we spend building what he calls our container. We develop our achievements, our identity, our job, our beliefs. The first half of life is the equivalent to what crawling is to babies, as in you don't want to stay crawling forever, but it typically comes before we can walk. Yet, only some make it to the second half. In the second half, we ask, what is this all for, and what do we do with it? He says most people don't make it to the questioning because they are addicted to their routines and busyness of the first half, so we need something to intervene and make it all fall apart. Necessary suffering that propels us to ask the hard questions of the second half, and in this space, if we can find grace and freedom, it moves us upward - but feels like falling.

In the middle of my spiritual crisis, I found comfort in his words, that my suffering was vital to understanding the full richness of God, even when it felt all wrong. It's counterintuitive to what I would have thought a spiritual journey to God would look like. It's for sure not something people share on Sundays from the pulpit.

In the months following the conference, and after reading *Falling Upward,* I knew I was in a transition phase. I didn't return to church regularly, but when I sat in the pews, I felt awkward and unable to muster confidence as my spiritual life was on pause. My past couldn't be unseen or unfelt or unknown. It was now part of me. But I could sense there was more I was missing. Everything to this point had me realizing how little about God I knew, and how much I'd gotten it wrong in the past. I didn't know how to move forward.

What happens when you can't go back to how things were before because you've lost your trust in the church? While I was stuck, everything else seemed to move forward. Lost and searching, I looked for the beautiful and broken and those who were waiting like me. I listened to strong women in my life. I also joined a Beth Moore Bible study, because it doesn't get much better than a God story told by Beth Moore. I read Barbara Brown Taylor, Shauna Niequist, and Anne Lamott. I also read every single book by Kristin Hannah because fiction sometimes is more real than reality.

I felt left behind and terrified at the idea of not having a religion. I cycled through the fuzziness, the empowering feeling of deciding things aren't what you've believed, and the sheer loneliness that falls after that.

I felt the push back when I spoke of my questioning about the church, religion, and God. A few times, I sat on my friend Sally's couch, wondering why it's so hard. She told me I need to decide if I can handle people stomping on my beliefs and said we have a lot of work to do. She reminded me that we have to keep feeling and loving and speaking the truth. I know she's right.

I'm tired of hiding. I've done this too long. This way of being, this living on the surface, staying in costume and pretending everything is perfect is no longer acceptable. The splintering down and dividing and side-picking has lost the thrill. I'm ready to search for the answers in the second half. I'm ready for the part when I stop feeling the need to self-protect and start looking beyond.

I decide to become a miner of the good like the gold rushers looking for something sparkly amongst the gray, dusty rocks and murky water. I need to learn the patient act of sifting and to taper the feeling of disappointment with the lack of resolution when I draw my pan from the water with nothing but pebbles and sharp stones. I need to learn the discipline of submerging it, again and again, working it back and forth with love and grace, all in search of a tiny sparkle. Right now, they are so small, I know if I'm not careful, I'll sift right though.

35. Just Downsizing

We were still waiting for military orders. The people who make the assignments, decisions, and hold power over our futures, are called detailers. They have to fill every job opening and, when they can, they will take into consideration a shortlist from the military member of their job and location preferences. Considering I can't even make a single dinner that makes both of my kids happy, I would never want this job. We all hope to get something on our wish list, but it doesn't always work out that way. In the end, they tell us where to move, and we pack our house and go there.

The few months between when Jeff turns in his shortlist and when we hear back from the detailers are pure torture. We live by the phone, waiting for the one call that will determine where we live for the next two to four years.

Years ago, right after I gave birth to Evan, while still in the hospital, Jeff went into work to see if his orders came in. It was *that* important. It becomes your sole purpose in life, waiting for that phone to ring with life-changing news, because your life will look very different if they send you to Hawaii versus Detroit versus New Orleans. So we waited and waited and waited. And just when I thought we couldn't wait anymore, we did. Until finally, Jeff called me. He was given a choice either of Maryland or the Dominican Republic. Both were on our list, so it wasn't entirely a shock. We talked about the pros and cons of each, but it was pretty much a no-brainer. He picked up the Dominican Republic job, which would send us back to Washington, D.C., for a year, before moving to the Caribbean.

Leaving Humboldt was bittersweet. We were energized for a new adventure and yet sad to leave the things we had grown to love. As luck would have it, on our last few days, an ugly, run-down RV parked right next to us. The couple living in the RV had tracks running up and down their arms. They would sleep all day and then around 10:00 pm start working on "remodeling" their RV, hammering right near where the boys' room was. We could not drive away fast enough.

So much good came from downsizing to a mere 375 square feet. We traveled, got outside more, and met a ton of interesting people. I made a life-long friendship, and the boys made memories, but it was far from the perfect life fix we were hoping for. Downsizing the physical stuff was the silver lining in all this, but you can't outrun life, and in life, there will always be hurdles. We can use the novelty of something new to fill a void, but you have to deal with the mental, emotional, and spiritual clutter. If not, it's like taking a giant box of clutter to donate at Goodwill and then picking up a box someone else's clutter on the way out.

We both have different opinions. If we could go back in time, I would still do it. Jeff said he wouldn't, which is understandable since he had to deal with the black tank.

We loaded the boys and hitched the truck to the RV. I found myself, for the second time, driving away from the West Coast towards the nation's capital. This time it wasn't towards my love because he was sitting next to me. I remembered back to that first drive and how anxious I was to see Jeff. I strategically stopped at a gas station a few miles away to put on a fresh layer of makeup and brush my teeth, but times have changed. My focus on the drive now was keeping the Kindles charged and entertainment running, and being the endless provider of goldfish and Cuties. And the gas station stops were for ushering in my kids who have to pee "right now." The last thing on my mind was makeup.

Exactly sixteen months to the very day, we moved out of the RV into a townhouse on Joint Base Anacostia-Bolling in D.C. We would have stayed in the RV longer, but there wasn't a good place to park the RV in the city. It was a relatively easy move, despite living in an empty house for a month because the military lost our shipment of the furniture we saved when moving into the RV. We sat on the floor to eat dinner and made weekly trips to the laundromat until the movers found our lost house shipment.

I loved being back in D.C.. Perhaps because I knew it was only for a year. We settled in quickly and got Evan enrolled in school. I started practicing Spanish, and Jeff started working.

On the first Sunday, we visited a church in the Navy Yard area about ten minutes from the base. It was on a busy city street full of restaurants and shops. We were greeted and told the children's church entrance was around the corner. We followed the tent signs around a few turns until I thought we were lost. Then I saw a church couple walking hand-in-hand into a building. My relief in finding the building was short-lived when I saw what the couple was wearing. He had on a suit with a tie, and she wore a long summer dress. Suddenly I was second-guessing my skinny blue jeans. I didn't remember D.C. churches being so formal.

"Do you think they dress up here?" I asked Jeff.

He shrugged his shoulders.

As we walked closer to the building the stylish couple had just entered, I saw the sign. Church of Jesus Christ of Latter-Day Saints. It was the wrong building.

We continued down the street and finally came across the kids' classroom and a pool of other jean-wearing-folk, and checked the boys into their classes. After, we made our way into the crowded service. It was held in a vintage theater, and every one of the deep red velvet seats was full. We were told this week's service was a little different than their regular church service. The topic was on hospitality, and being a good neighbor, and making connections to people who aren't like us. Although Jesus was mentioned less than other churches, the loving way they spoke of meeting others felt utterly like Jesus.

We liked the Navy Yard church but didn't want to commit without trying a few others in the area. The next Sunday, we decided to go back to the church we had attended when we lived in D.C. before. It was hot and muggy, but the drive was fast and parking easy to find. After the kids checked in to their classes, Jeff and I walked into the large, air-conditioned sanctuary and took seats towards the back. It didn't surprise me that I sat next to someone in marathon training gear. D.C. people are such overachievers. It was dark, and the band was playing "This Is How I Fight My Battles" with concert-quality production and green and blue strobe lights. I think I saw a fog machine. There was security walking around, and a police officer at the front door. It made me feel better with all the church shootings recently. As I listened to the announcements, I noted how much the church had grown since we were here last. They had seemingly perfected every part of the service. Nothing was left untouched. Despite the fact, Jeff and I attended this church for nearly three years before we moved, we saw not one familiar face. Even the pastor was new.

The perfect worship, the thoughtfulness of the greeters and endless activities to get involved, was everything I craved in a church the last five years since we moved away, and yet, it felt entirely wrong. It seemed to be crafted and planned in a way to evoke a particular emotion or response. Even the TV timer in the lobby was counting down the seconds until the next "experience." It felt like a marketing attempt crafted to allow the feeling of the Holy Spirit. Everything I had missed was making me incredibly uncomfortable, with the exception, of course, the Starbucks coffee bar in the lobby. When did they get this?

As a church summer schedule would have it, and the same as the Navy Yard church, a guest pastor led the service. We left feeling disconnected but decided to try again the next week. By the second week, our boys had fallen in love with the children's church. There's a decent amount of military mom guilt when you routinely uproot your children, and the fact they were enjoying church sealed our decision to keep coming back. We wanted a church space where the boys would make friends and get to know the Sunday school teachers.

We rarely missed a week, and the topics sparked great conversations for Jeff and me. Some weeks we agreed with the church, and some weeks we didn't. They continued to rotate pastors, and each one had their own style. I liked how much they focused on living positive, encouraging others, and pushing the idea of how much you believe in God matters less than what kind of God you believe in. I liked the saying that when we sit in exile and seek the promised land with our whole hearts, it will descend on us.

Of course, there were things I could live without, like during worship, the pastors from stage yelling at us to "Clap our hands for Jesus." It didn't bother me before, but now it annoyed me. At times I felt God and the Bible were misrepresented, and it made me question the entire logic of the teaching. There were a lot of certainties and blanket statements used when interpreting God's word, which seemed to leave little room for questions. Like one Sunday when the pastor repeated a few times, that "The word of God always demands a response." There are many ways to read into this, but does the word of God actually always demand a response? Where is the contemplation in that? Maybe the contemplation is a response. I don't know.

Another thing I heard, familiar among evangelicals that, as they say, gets my goat, is the notion that we don't deserve God. "He'll rescue us even though we don't deserve Him." It always seems to contrast with the other notion that we are beloved children of God and who brings children into the world without loving them? If you birth a child into the world, that child deserves love.

In the hours I sat in church, frustrated, uncomfortable, and, at times, angry, I acknowledged how deep my church wounds had grown over the last ten years. I felt like a fish out of water, but I went back every Sunday. I knew there was something I could learn from this situation. Plus, I think I mentioned, there was a Starbucks.

I learned a crucial thing. I didn't belong there. After weeks of showing up and listening, being cynical to a fault, I realized how judgmental I was towards how others are choosing to be in the way of the church. I wondered, just because it was different for me, could I learn to respect and appreciate this, for them? I learned I needed to grow my sense of love for these church people, and maybe even, one day, give up the idea they should be different.

In the years past, my cry was for the church to be more tolerant and inclusive, and yet I had grown so intolerant of other Christians. I had wanted the church to be okay with the wonder and mystery of God, and I was mad they had become lost in their search for certainty. But I was falling to see that many, many people come to these very churches and find that wonder and mystery and just because I wasn't finding it for myself, in the same way, I was doing a great disservice in my harsh judgments of the very place I used to love so much.

The most significant part of my pain didn't come from my difference in theology. The most significant part of my pain came from letting the theology separate me from other people. I needed to reclaim love for people whom I don't agree with. The only way I knew to do that was by continuing to show up every week. Proximity would push me into restoration, and learning to love better would be to remove the distance between them and me. Hopefully.

Speaker Peter de Jager wrote, "The Zulu greeting, 'Sawubona' means 'I see you,' and the response 'Ngikhona' means 'I am here.' As always, when translating from one language to another, crucial subtleties are lost. Inherent in the Zulu greeting and our grateful response, is the sense that until you saw me, I didn't exist. By recognizing me, you brought me into existence. A Zulu folk saying clarifies this, 'Umuntu ngumuntu nagabantu,' meaning, 'A person is a person because of other people'."

I've gotten skilled at not seeing people from the church I grew up in — not one church building specifically but the collective church. I exclude people who are too loud about their unbending beliefs. I exclude people who are too quiet and don't speak up for those being hurt. People who are too popular, too antisocial, too young, too old, too many problems, no problems. I've carefully deduced and written these people off as one, and only one thing, as I failed to acknowledge the rich depth in all people.

And yet, I want to have the kind of eyes that see everyone and think they belong to me, because if I can't see others as belonging to me, then I will never belong to them. I want to collect people the way the ocean collects shells. All shapes. All colors. All beliefs about the world. All beautiful. I want to find a connection with people not based on how much common theology we have, but because we both have a beating heart. I want to give up the loneliness for belonging.

I've come to realize in nearly all my circles, people feel they don't belong. We are too different from our families, our coworkers, our friends, our communities. Feeling like we don't belong had become a lifestyle choice of loneliness because by thinking, "I don't belong," we give ourselves validation in not sharing our hearts and being vulnerable. But belonging is a birthright. We know this because we were born. We are here. Simple, but it's everything.

My ego wants me to confirm before I pour my heart out, that others will stand next to me in support. There's no guarantee for this, but I can choose to do this for others, and for myself, by returning the gift of freedom and acceptance. And to be okay with who we are at the moment and the grace to grow into something new. It's in this place, I hope to find a new story where belonging and connection triumph over the loneliness of a faith shift.

I decided to attend the IF:Gathering that year in Annapolis. As I walked into the beautiful room, I noticed the work that went into making this happen. The vibe was J. Crew meets Anthropologie because, Annapolis. I was apprehensive but hopeful. While I missed Friday's speakers, I appreciated Saturday's program. Coming into this space with a bit more compassion for myself and others let me walk away feeling at peace and freedom to move on to my next chapter.

36. Gazpacho

I hate gazpacho. It's finicky and terrible. If you don't know what gazpacho is, I'll tell you, and you might hate it too. It's raw vegetables, usually tomatoes, blended and served cold. They call it soup, and this is where my problem lies. In my world, there is no such thing as a cold soup. Tomatoes pureed and served cold is so clearly ketchup, although some might argue that ketchup should be room temperature, which is highly irrelevant in this case. To be called soup, it must be at least 150 degrees. I think it's in the Constitution. But people ignore this. They pour cold ketchup in a soup bowl, serve it with a soup spoon, and call it gazpacho. The indecisiveness is the reason I hate gazpacho. It's wishy-washy. You're either soup, or you're ketchup. You cannot be both.

At my best friend's bachelorette party, on the drive from the winery to the restaurant, I was asked by another more conservative party-goer, "Angela, are you a Christian?"

I froze. It wasn't a hard question, but I didn't know how to answer, and I shrugged it off and stuttered, "Um, maybe." Deep breath. "Uh, well, not in the traditional way, I mean, I don't know that by many traditional Christians standards, I would qualify anymore."

My best friend, buzzed as she was, said, "I think you are."

I laughed, and we changed the subject. But this quick interaction had me thinking later on. At the moment when prompted, I didn't feel I had permission to call myself a Christian because others would tell me I was wrong or not saved or wishy-washy on the truth. Some might even say I am the gazpacho of Christianity.

Asked again, without hesitation, I would say yes and hope I didn't feel the need to explain myself. Many of my traditional evangelical friends might say I'm not a Christian because I've downsized the fundamentals. I'm okay with this. I will no longer stop speaking up because someone might not agree with me or say I'm not Christian enough.

I'm past cute religious phrases like, "it's not a religion - it's a relationship." I'm over talk of "winning people to the kingdom" and Christians who are "set apart." Jaded? Perhaps. Pissed? At times. But if I could move past this, and sometimes I can, I would say choosing Christ means we have a calling to live better than we are currently, while simultaneously being content as we are, and moving through the world with a confidence and peace, while learning to separate ourselves from the ugliness and lies that depreciate or disesteem us as less than, not enough, or too much, anything that tells us we need others approval, or anything other than what we were already born with to be complete. We stop measuring our lives by our achievements, our power, and our fancy belongings, and throw out the entire loser yardstick. This act makes us perfect in weakness.

Weakness is our most beautiful element. When we allow love to meet weakness, our fragility and susceptibility to criticism, loneliness, and inadequacy are blocked by our fierceness to love others, our courage to take a stand exactly where we are, and our heart to make a difference in the world. Weakness is what stretches us. Being pulled is not something we can do passively. Michelangelo said, "Every block of stone has a statue inside it, and it is the task of the sculptor to discover it." I believe it's both me and God, co-sculptors of my heart, together chipping away each little piece of shame, contempt, and heartache to reveal my true, whole self.

The barriers of a peaceful life, like hopelessness, scarcity, pride, shame about our past, poor body image, fear of being judged or judging others, keep us from fully reaching God.

But by deciding to do the hard work of sorting all this out and growing our emotional intelligence, we get an authentic glimpse of God in the process. Most of the time, we might feel incomplete and wrestle with one issue or another, but we find God in pressing forward.

I believe the only way we live out this calling is with other people, meeting them where they are, not to "win them for the kingdom," but to treasure them. We live it out by being sad about what makes God sad - hatefulness. And loving what God loves - people.

My spiritual crisis isn't something that needs healing. Churches that promote submission and traditional marriage, churches who misinterpreted scripture, and coat abuse with words like submission - it's these places that need healing. During the last decade, I've felt the uncertainty with the church. I've mourned, and I've let go of many beliefs I held as absolute truth. It's brought me to a place of endless critical questions, including my place in the church. And yet more peace than ever with the paradoxes of God.

This moment isn't my whole life, but a tiny piece. It doesn't tie in a pretty bow. It's not over yet. My biggest challenge has been unpacking my spiritual standings, letting go of bitterness towards the church, and learning to love better. Writing about my first marriage, abuse, and the connection with fundamentalism and sexism in the church has been heavy. There was a time when I let the hurt from one terrible church season trickle into all areas of my life, but that time is mostly gone. However, this didn't morph me back into the person I was before, even as hard as I once prayed for it. I don't sit in church with an open wound but a scar through which I see differently, at times more critically, but mostly I strive to see a bigger picture and the example of who Christ is.

I'm reminded that Jesus was a peacemaker, not a peacekeeper. Some areas of the church are seriously flawed — some ideas beyond repair. We need to continue to speak about these. But mostly the people behind them are good, want to do good, and see the good. I believe we are all doing the best we can. My mentor Jody Moore says, "Some people's best is truly terrible, but it's their best." Maybe they need to believe this right now. Perhaps it's helpful for them to believe this. I know personally. I've gone through the wringer losing aspects of my faith, and it's lonely, and you get rejected, and people don't understand. There are times I'm happy for them because they seem surer of themselves than I am.

If you're in a spiritual crisis, I will offer you this. Just because it's not life-giving now, doesn't mean it won't be ever again. And even more true, just because it helped last week, doesn't mean it will always be the only answer.

Ultimately, I get to decide how I want to guide my life. When fear is guiding me, I react from a place of anger, contempt, and shame. When love is my guide, I can teach myself to see God in all things and all people. I think this is the purest form of abundance.

The Bible can seem scary at times. But when I read,

"God is love, and whoever abides in love, abides in God, and God abides in him (her)." 1 John 4:16

Or, "So now faith, hope, and love abide, these three; but the greatest of these is love."

That doesn't seem so scary. *It's beautiful, actually.*

Acknowledgements

To Jeff, Evan, and Ethan. You are my everything.

To my mom, who taught me grumpy people might just be having a bad day.

To my dad, who served nearly 40 years in the Navy and parented with dad jokes and the command hand known to all military kids.

To my sister, Christie, for her love, encouragement, and strawberry Jello cake.

To my aunties and the women in my family who gather and comfort.

To my mother-in-law, Julie, for her wisdom and for raising a strong and wise son.

To Stefanie for telling me to shave my face and be nice to my husband and being my ride-or-die.

To Leslie for weathering the treacherous talks about faith and life with a dose of humor and love.

To Emily for our eight-year-old selves and now watching our boys play together.

To Nikki for your open perspective and encouragement.

To Marina and Mike for your support and love.

To Susan Coffman Reams and Lanette Dickerson for teaching me how to vacation, make cinnamon rolls, and including me in your family.

To my editor Beth Richardson who transformed my words into something readable and partnered with me to bring this book to the world.

To my mentor and friend, Kathi Lipp, you have been such an example of great leadership, generosity, and God's love.

To my business coach and friend, Tonya Kubo, for seeing the potential in this downsizing message. You are such a gift.

To those who helped me draw out my message. Especially Shantell Brightman, Cheri Gregory, Lori Young, Kelly Wilbanks, Stefanie Fargo, and Angela Bouma.

To Rachelle Gardner for our coaching session and giving me a giant helping of motivation, encouragement, and nudging me in the right direction.

To my life coach, Natalie Clay, my deepest gratitude for the work we did together.

To the strong women I've worked for and learned from—especially Maggie Lahr, Nadette Bishop, Maggie Jones, and Marti Watson Garlett.

To the women at church whose kindness is a big reason I waited with the church during my faith wrestling. Notably, the Grove girls, Sheri, Julie, Stephanie, and Gina; and in Humboldt Debbie Parks, Cheryl Crackel Turner, and Kay Richardson Libolt.

For all the women who have blessed me as I've moved coast to coast, in San Diego, D.C., Poulsbo, Humboldt, and all over the map. There are too many to name, but I'm deeply honored to have you in my life. Especially Michelle, Sally, Maggie, Krystal, Crystal, Martha, Danielle, Amber, and AshleyAnn.

For my Writing at the Red House cohort, teachers, and friends, Susy Flory, Anna LeBaron, Kelly Wilbanks. Debbie Kitterman, Margaret

Lalich, Priscila L. Sharrow, and Dorthy Strouhal. I'm honored to be a part of this writer's space.

To the late Rachel Held Evans for being there when my faith was unraveling.

To my real heroes, my kids' teachers and babysitters, there would be no book without them.

Made in the USA
Middletown, DE
29 September 2020